Moonlight Magic

By

Hector L Espinosa

Contents

Chapter 1	Natural order	page 3
Chapter 2	By the numbers	page 34
Chapter 3	Stories	page 78
Chapter 4	Healing ways	page 135
Chapter 5	Personal visions	page 180

www.heaven2earth.info

Copyright 2014

Order this book through www.heaven2earth.info

You may also order:

Life & Beyond

Light and the Darkness

Through this site as well as major book retailers.

You may find all of these books through on line retailers for your tablet as well.

**Chapter 1
Natural Order**

The world was created by energies we still don't completely understand, we are but a speck of dust in this Universe. It's through our small understanding of our surroundings that the spark of life can be re-lit. Many eons have passed since we humans begun our existence in this wondrous world called earth. Our understanding has ebbed in and out like the oceans throughout our time. There have been brief moments where a few have learned to tap this energy called magic. Remember it's just a word for what we do not understand but it will be part of the natural order of things. Since the beginning humans have because of fear destroyed what was feared. Not too long ago witches were burned because of what was considered dangerous by those ignorant enough to fear the unknown. It's because of this fear that humanity has lost knowledge that if passed down our enlightment would have been light years ahead of what it is today. The watered down version of what was once discovered and lost has trickled down to us today.

Today there are many books about so called magic, some empathize spiritual magic, other material magic as done through cauldron's and offerings to deities older than time itself. Instead of fearing these unknown what needs to happen is like in science, experimentation and through practice unlock age old secrets to better the human condition. I myself have over the last 15 years of practicing these ancient beliefs have been able to do what humans today call magic. Imagine how science has expanded its knowledge of the human condition even through biology allow many women unable to conceive to give birth to healthy children. There are limits to science even in this as many have failed to get pregnant or even maintain this to conception but there are alternatives. I've had the pleasure over these many years to achieve beyond the limits of today's science and manifested success with some of these women through natural some call magical means; allowing these otherwise infertile women to conceive, over 15 times and with great ease these women who have failed after many thousands of dollars and years of trial and failure to gain what they wished for most, get pregnant and give natural birth.

Given the right circumstances we as humans may achieve sometimes in addition to science more than science alone can master. I'm not against science for it's just another name but still within the natural order of things. All existence is part of the natural order, in this book I would like to open eyes to this concept and perhaps create an understanding that there are no limits to what we can accomplish if we but open our minds and hearts that there is no impossibility only limitations set upon ourselves. Break these barriers and the imagination is our only limit, this concept is the one true limit, that there are none beyond what is achievable if we but believe. Give me an open mind and what you can accomplish will even astonish the most incredulous person amongst us. Life does not feel real unless others are watching seems to happen to many; I believe deep in our subconscious we have a need for logic, for things to make sense, unfortunately we live in a world that is often beyond logic, beyond sense.

I believe reality leaves a lot to the imagination, it's a series of spontaneous changes, stop resisting because life is not a problem to be solved, its often filled with inaccuracies not to be micromanaged but experienced! Stop looking for the meaning of life of happiness for it's not ready-made rather it comes from each of your actions. It's impossible to protect yourself from sadness without protecting yourself from happiness; caution in love is the most fatal to true happiness. Start everyday inspired to do better, meet and overcome all obstacles, all challenges, know you are alive for a purpose, the purpose is fluid and changes as you grow, so row your boat to the next shore, to the next adventure and become all you can be in this life! Stay away from basing happiness on another's opinion or expectation; it's always better to climb your ladder of success, instead of being at the top that others say is right. Create your life, the life that feels right and be in your own happy place. Freedom to realize everyone does not have to like you and you don't have to like everyone, if they say you've changed is that a bad thing or is it they realized you stopped living their way; so don't let the bitterness of others change you, it's their loss if they can't value what you're worth.

I recall last year on one of my many visits to the Hamptons I was introduced to the brother of one of my clients companion. This was a man that life had delved many difficult blows and was not much of a believer in anything even God or the concept of a God was outside the realm of possibilities. I was hesitant to speak with him as my basic concept is simply if you want to be helped by me you need only ask. This was at that time beyond the belief system of this individual; after a little coaxing by my client and her boyfriend I agreed to do a cleansing for him. He was very polite but politely told me he was not a believer in anything I or anyone else practiced. I decided to help him in the one way I could, to open his mind and heart that there was more out there than his experience had proven to him. The foundation for Love is friendship, honesty, character, integrity, faith, loyalty, it's that understanding through good and bad times, forgiving and settling for less than perfection, making allowances for human weakness! The game of life demands loyalty, responsibility, virtue, faithfulness; in return you receive fulfillment and peace of mind.

I reminded him of how often good friendships can become intimate. On the other side of that coin is co-dependency jealousy, self-esteem issues or ego; no matter how well we intellectualize this, our hearts can unwittingly continue on a path to destroy what we value the most. If he wanted to close escrow on that elusive long lasting relationship that sometimes seems so close he could taste it and all of the sudden the ego steps in and causes damage. I told him to make a conscious decision to cancel jealousy's ugly head from rearing and see the person as they truly are and not as his self-projection from the ego that causes the problems in the first place.

I began by explaining to him how I worked and every cleansing was different so for him I would do one with cigar. I showed him a regular everyday cigar still in its wrapper and I told him I would as he was sitting in a chair pass this smoke all around him as I did the cigar would burn in different ways and I would be able to read it much like some read tea leaves in a cup. He looked at me in disbelief but was patient with what I was sure he was thinking so much nonsense. As I began I asked him about people from his past, before I began I had prayed on the best way to help him and decided to work on his past present and future. I prayed that the information I would be shown was also outside the scope of knowledge his brother had of him so he would not think I was told these things to fool him. My initial talk with him was about a long ago girlfriend and what had happened to them in the relationship. I told him things that I could see by his demeanor were interesting. I realized early on in the cleaning that he was barren, barren to believe in love so I also gave him plenty of food 4 thought about that topic. I reminded him not to hold back, give what you can, never allow yourself to be used, listen but don't lose your own voice, speak your truth, remember negative people and their opinions with time can derail your destiny; don't worry kindness is not weakness, nor is forgiveness acceptance, keep in mind resentment and regret is the true enemy.

He began to sit up and he uncross his legs and the defensive posture relaxed as I continued with other events in his past that not even the family knew had happened to him. We discussed events as If I had partaken in them, I could tell by that point he was baffled as to who I was and how I knew these things. I tell you this but he did not utter a word, just answered my questions and we discussed events and I gave him my take on them offering a different view but all made perfect sense. His eyes would squint at some of the concepts I would bring up and described people in great detail as to hair color what they did and how they acted in different scenarios as he lived them. When he started to dialogue back with me I knew he was hooked. By the end of the cleanse it was as if we had known each other for a lifetime. I gave him many forecasted events that were to come to pass within a year or so.

It wasn't until a year later when I saw the family again that they told me I had changed his life and he had become himself again a new man with hopes and dreams as he had confided in them that most of what I had forecasted had come to pass. You must remember the object of what I do is give faith so your lives will have the meaning it was intended in the first place. I don't change any destinies but make it the best it can be allowing nature to take its natural path for each life I touch. No such thing as things going outside this; life is as I've come to describe it in 90 degrees. If on the left you are in mud and nothing works out for you. If on the right it seems like you are walking on water, in the middle is where most lives propagate. So if a person that is living the negative side of their possibility comes to me and I move them to the middle or God forbid the right, it sure seems like magic but still within the realm of what the person's natural destiny was to be in the first place. If you want to put all that I want to explain in my books into a simple description this is it.

Your soul chooses the life, within this there is always 90 degrees of separation, it is that small amount of space that all things can be changed; does not matter, spiritual, Feng Shui or any other form or description of modality, including medicine, when it's your time that's it and all the medicine in the world won't change that. With that being said, if you are living a life on the left or negative side of your existence and get a disease then medicine can cure but only because you were supposed to be cured. If on the other hand it's your time to die, let's face it, death is as natural a part of us as life then we die no matter what. Just think objectively of the person in a horrific car crash that survives and the person that trips, falls and dies from an aneurism. Why those extremes, well that is life attempting to assert itself and on the other hand death also takes its toll when it's time.

We begin to truly live life when we stop fearing it, so open your mind and heart; start to expand your Universe, its mighty big and definitely has room for you and all your friends and family closed off to magic. Some would say no one can have everything they want, for goodness sake where will they ever put it. Make room because these concepts will allow you to grow and grow until adding another room might not be enough then we add more land and build more room. The idea is as big as your imagination will grow it, the limits are, well I have not found them yet. We use a small portion of our minds, let's expand them and fill it with more of everything all that fertile mind space going to waste. The more we know the more we want to know and the more ideas come to light and growth is inevitable. Truth is self-sustaining, it will stand the test of time, be just and we will prevail through any adversity, be loyal to ourselves and others when deserved; simply treat others as you would be treated and loyalty you will attain!

The spiritual mass!

No one has all the answers so some come to people like me for some of the possibilities. I tell my clients to listen and if it makes sense then give it value if not there is always a choice and I recommend choosing not to listen. Recently I was invited to a spiritual mass, in these there are usually several people like me, remember no one has all the answers, no one medium can see everything, the more evolved the higher, further out the person can see. So I was invited along with several other mediums, I did not know any of them so it was exiting for me, the lady who asked for this was a client who was going through a rough patch. She believed that something, harm was done to her by someone else.

I recall the reading she had with me and I did not perceive this but agreed with her that two eyes are better than one and six are even better. This was how many mediums she had contacted to come. In these events one needs to be prepared for the unexpected. No one truly knows what is to happen and I was the outsider as it seemed like the rest of them knew each other. Again I was happy as I'm usually the one who does these or at the very least sets them up; an opportunity to so others do their thing.

She wanted me to be the one who kept an eye on the happenings just in case something did not seem right I should let her know. I'm sure she had this in mind but most of these sessions are very cool and the majority of the people who preside over them are just like me, people who have the calling and truly want to help. As the session started there were many prayers and such to get the ambiance flowing. So far meeting most of the people before we started I got a good feeling from the experience. So as the lady who presided organized where all were to be seated she told me she wanted me to sit on the other corner. This is usually done with the person in need at the center and facing a wall with a table and white cloth covering the table; remember the representation of white here is purity, new fresh. She is placed looking at the table; this table usually has some flowers, white and many cups of water to help in the absorption of energy from the event and one or more candles.

Underneath her one glass filled with water and a small candle next to it or inside the water. I prefer inside but this was more traditional so on the side. The session always starts with doing a thou father prayer and invoking the session for good and God to preside and look out for all of us. Remember most of these mediums can channel and with the person in the middle any one can pick up negative energy or a negative obsessive spirit from the person. This is part of the reason for the gathering and the other to unravel any messages from her own spirits as to why she is going through such difficult times. The client told me the lady who is presiding is who she regularly goes to for counseling. I liked her energies and she seemed to know what she was doing.

I must remind you that when practicing any sort of esoteric art you must always be clear on intent, this stuff is serious and to play around with any magic can be dangerous. To practice without a clear understanding of what you are doing can cause great harm to yourself or others, all this is if you are doing good. So you must understand doing bad or evil or working any magic from a dark place can bring on very negative entities and very destructive results so stay in the light and practice with care. The importance when practicing magic is to be very careful with negative entities especially when channeling the spiritual realm. When practicing black magic, demonology, Satanism, or other pagan religion or practice we must be vigilant; magic isn't a game and should never be taken lightly. You never know what's on the other side and the effects it might have could very well affect not only self but those loved ones in your life.

At first the lady who ran the session told me she and I would be the two ends to the semi-circle. I thought it curious since she did not know me but I got it and said sure. We were the strongest two in the group and would be the correct people to run shotgun as it were. Remember there always have to be responsible spirits to protect the rest or at the very least if the stuff gets ugly take over and keep control. I guess from her perspective that would be her or me. We continued with the prayers and every once in a while one of the mediums would call out something they saw, so it was for about thirty minutes until I decided this was a good group and I had let them run for a while. I started to speak as well. Don't get me wrong I was doing prayer all along to keep the energies clean and flowing allowing others to do their thing.

Someone had mentioned a spirit with certain tendencies I concurred and added how that is or was the spirit who would help this woman find a good husband. Another medium confirmed this and we continued, remember the idea was to uncover her spirits and give their messages. In this type of session there is always one who writes everything down so the person can review and as the messages continued believe me you will want to do this as after a while there could be 20 or more pages of messages and things the person has to do in order to get rid of obstacles.

Working with all these fine mediums we were with time able to discover a spirit who I had detailed as a spirit that made her cry and keep her emotionally spent. The lady who was sitting next to me was the one who took on the entity and as we worked to get it to understand to move one and leave her alone it tried to get close to the person in the middle we prevented it from doing this and it got angry. After some heavy prayer and communicating with the entity it finally left. I believe she will now be alleviated from these moments of sadness, according to her would last a day or more when they hit her.

Many good things where done on her behalf on this day including her channeling two of her own spirits and gave messages to some of the folks that were there. Remember spirits have gifts and each according to their evolution can help the living so always stay open to messages. As the session came to an end I was very pleased on how this would play out for the lady and she looked refreshed so we all felt the job was done. Some final prayers and we closed the session, after she gave us some food as is customary to give thanks for the session that had occurred.

What do you see if you look at zero, nothing; but if you look through it, if you stayed faithful to the light you will carry the torch to light the next generation, become the leader and realize what is Leadership if not the ability to lift and inspire. Join the team, God's team of light and inspire those around you! Surprising you will find the affection connection, how friends and love ones can heal the world around them. Keep in mind being loved gives us strength but loving someone deeply gives us the courage to realize that hate is too great a burden to bear and ultimately takes us into the darkness. While we work to create light for others we've learned to light our own way, open other's door and life will open your doors! Free yourself from life's dramas, simplify by looking inward and remember, if you've got nothing to say it's okay abstain from speaking the nonsense that will proof that fact!

Clear spaces of negative energies

I'm a firm believer to clean the energies of the home, so here is a good one; take a wide mouth wine glass, no designs on the glass or colors. Fill it with water and add the white of an egg, start from the back forwards or from the second floor down if there is one. Start by choosing the room furthest to the back and come forward to the last room by the front door. So once a day you will take the wine glass and fill with fresh water, tap water is fine, and then add the white of the egg into the water. Try and place it always in the highest position in each room, for example in the kitchen at least over the refrigerator. As you raise the glass over your head to place it ask for the commission of spirits that clears spaces to clear the space surrounding this room of any negative energy, always in God's name.

 The next morning you take the glass and flush its contents down the toilet. Waste not is my motto so get the yellow of the egg, don't throw it out, place it in a cup and save in the refrigerator. Once you have at least three yokes add one spoon of honey, one of olive oil, mix all together and add to your damaged hair. I like to say at least an hour with a shower cap then go to the sink and wash off with beer, at least three cans full of beer. Rinse it all off and go take a shower, shampoo and condition your hair then you are good to go. While on the subject you can do a cleansing of the head with avocado, if you look down you will find the how in detail. It will not only cool your thought proses but in the doing your hair will look and feel better.

Continue to do this room by room until you arrive to the last room, usually the living room and always the next morning clean the glass add the fresh water and a new egg must be broken to attain the fresh white of the egg and insert into the glass full of water. Always ask for the same thing as the first room and you continue until complete. Once you do this you will take a box of incense sticks and place one in each room in the home and burn them. You can do the same thing on the exterior, place all over the sides of the home. If you live in a place you cannot place them all around the 360 degrees of the house you may just place them at the entrance. The object is like cleaning your house, if you don't after a while the place is dirty so energy is the same and if you maintain clean the flow of energy will always be at its best. Like all energy if you do the same thing over and over eventually it will stop working, if you think of this as an antibiotic your doctor will tell you if you keep on using the same one eventually your body will get used to it and no longer will it have an effect.

So here are some other simple ways to keep the energy flow, try getting a gallon of white vinegar and in each of the four corners of every single room sprinkle a little and let it air dry. So simply pour a little in each corner and continue until you hit the last room by the front door. After you are done pour the rest out the front door and again the important part is to let it air dry. If you have rug then pour baking soda on the rug and leave it on for a day or so before you vacuum it clean. Another popular is smudging or using a sage stick and walk the entire house from back to front as you walk blow on it and ask to cleanse the area, remember the corners are important so make sure you blow onto each of the four corners of every room and also on all the windows and doorways. No matter if the doors or windows are closed remember we are cleaning energy so the blocks we are attempting to open are spiritual so a physical door or window will not interfere. Now that you have the idea you may use any and all of your own ways to do this ritual that should be done once a month, if the place is already stagnant maybe once a week for a month then continue once a month.

The magic of this world is love in everything around us, the beauty of creation, if we but took the time to breathe it in realizing we love because we need is not enough however we need because we love is the one true love that can be shared with all around us. Become a good listener and open the door to communication, to flow, accept the magic the love all around us and not just the love we think we deserve. Pose this question in front of the mirror, can you see magic, can you see love, bring this thought along with it, can we see the wind, is it there, so is love so is magic. Love is the only tangible emotion that may heal us fully after devastation of any sort! Remember yesterday is not yours to recover, tomorrow is yours to win; you believed just yesterday you could not live without them, now it's plain as day how easy it was to do so give yourself some wiggle room for change. Don't snub contentment for spectacular, remember a flying star is impressive, spectacular even that's why so many covet it, unfortunately it burns out quickly, and contentment lasts a lifetime!

Fate's premise is because it is and acknowledging it does not change its purpose so acceptance is part of this proses. We must be able to embrace life at its worse in order to deserve it at its best. Most of us reject happiness simply because we do not deserve it, rewire this train of thought and the world of magic will be yours. We deserve because we exist not for our accomplishments or any other tangible measurement. Use prayer, this form of self-help will keep you grounded not to influence God with requests but simply as a self-reminder when we waver that he walks with us all. It's truly a gift if you but allow others to give to you and your truest appreciation is in the acceptance of such a gift with gratitude in your heart, so be it, be grateful accept the gifts of living remember gracious acceptance is an art, cultivate it, allow another to express their feelings for you! Life is an eternal risk, some you win and happy you will be and good memories you will create, others you will lose and wiser you will become from lessons learned, but to live you must play the game of life!

Do not lose faith in humanity do not fear, trust that our fate is ours; a gift bestowed upon each of us and therefore cannot be taken except by our own self-doubt! I'm spending time discussing these concepts because so many of us lack the faith to see nature for what it is, a bounty filled with magic. Such concepts as life and death deter us from self-growth, remember life as death is but a passing from one room to another; each lifetime is like school, some classes are just more interesting while others we have to repeat until we learn the lesson! We must do the right thing not because by doing so we will be saved but because it's the right thing to do and your nature connection will open and that magic will reveal itself. It's funny, how frightening to let someone in to your most secret self, yet we are alone without it, you've wanted to be let into another's innermost self yet when it happens you are nervous feeling then you would have to give it up as well, we all long to be let in and to let in, let go and be free to become part of that most private space, share and be shared, don't fear!

Without hope, confidence, optimism and faith we are lost as the road darkens with despair and self-doubt, remember faith and prayer are the vitamins to our soul! Faith and patience are two essentials we must never waiver from as we travel this magical world for even when we try and fail perseverance will carry us to success. Sometimes we feel unequal to the task, we say what difference can I make, can a prayer make, well let's look; what difference can a mosquito make in your room at night, or an ant in your clothing, or a bee sting. Get the picture, maybe one prayer won't, but many over a period of time will make all the difference in the world, therefore you can make a big difference in your life or any other life. Never give up, usually what is coming has a chance of being better, dwelling on negatives will only determine your future failures. Let your mistakes become your motivators; remember it's how you deal with your past that predicts your future. Step by step move forwards and you will eventually be surprised how far you can go from what you thought was the end!

There are different types of magic, earth, water; well you know the elements so if working in the forest keep it simple use those ingredients. While at a river keep it related to the area you are working with, of course the stars can always be included to boost your chances to succeed. For example on the night of the full moon you may work abundance spells same with the new moon releasing type spells are used. It's important to use all magic spells with nature, in other words stay away from manmade stuff such as plastics or ink from pens rather use pencils and brown paper bags instead of white treated paper.

We cannot have everything or can we, where would you put it, don't worry with knowledge comes understanding and along with it comes more room to grow after all we use but a small percentage of our minds, imagine all the fertile mind space yet to farm. Within our minds we possess all that was, is and will be so tapping into it is all we need in order to achieve the magic that is existence. In order to achieve some measure of success in dong magic we must reconnect down to basics, down to nature's bounty. This can mean we must rewire what a lifetime of negative emotions and impressions have damaged in us. So I must recap what is nature in order to proceed.

Patience and understanding is essential to achievement so if you are willing to take the journey disappointment will not be your companion rather a sense of wonder and excitement as every step brings you closer to that simple connection with the divine. We are product of our past, don't be jailed by it, changing of your mind is part of growth, it's ok to change direction, grow and become more than the sum of your experiences. Expect less, have patience, with time we realize what's needed and what we should leave behind; focus on what's holding you together not on what's tearing you apart. Life will either bear sweet fruit you will enjoy or teach you when it's time to move on; have patience everything in life comes to pass sooner or later!

 Some would say that our existence is based on the knowledge we possess free will, but what if this entire foundation was based on a half-truth only. Much like we believe that in this big universe there is but one people and we are it. A bit narcissistic I would say for in the billions of stars out there how can we be the only planet with some sort of life. We can further take this process to believe we are the only intelligent life out there. If we can at the very least acknowledge that control is an illusion, what I mean that at best we can control how we feel about a situation and not the actual ability to control it or the person causing our discomfort if that were the case then we would be half way into understanding my topic of destiny or free will. We must learn to step out of our own way, like the snake we must shed our path as we outgrow ours; else we become obsolete like the discarded skin of the snake who grew beyond its current surroundings!

Can we truly say that things are random; or is there cause and effect and if there is this cause and effect then can we further understand that predetermined events are set into motion with or without our acting upon them. For example, the sun will shine in the morning if we are up to observe it or not. The moon will show itself even if we fell asleep before it came out. If we do not fill our gas tanks will we not run out of gas and therefore be late for work. I'd say there are some events that no matter how hard we might want to change them will come to fruition. Can we also accept this in our own lives, we cannot control another's life path, and eventually as individuals we will act according to our nature and not as others would have us do. If we dwell on the creation of a perfect tomorrow we might forget to live today, count your blessings, take a break; the trick to no regret is in enjoying today and not wishing it gone for a better tomorrow.

The idea of this conversation is that predetermined events concept is not completely wrong, in fact many of our plans are predetermined and to such a degree that even today science has been able to observe that we make up our minds before cognitive mind realizes it. For example in a study people were given random impute and asked to choose. Some were shown a colored cloth, and scientifically proven we made the choice of the favorite color way in advance before making the selection. In our D.N.A. there is a path that our minds and bodies will choose irrelevant to free will. So if this insignificant test proves that we are predetermined for certain things then might it not also lead us to believe that we are guided to choose who to marry or what job to take, even how to raise our children irrelevant to our formal education. As my wife likes to say, we will be what we will regardless of what we are taught.

Such concepts are scary and most do not speak of this because of the destructive effects that it could have on society. A society driven by the fact that anything can cause a specific effect and we control this outcome to a certain degree. What we have just discussed is contrary to this belief and in fact only the most fundamental of outcomes are really within our scope of influence and determinism will shine as the overall winner in this battle for decision making. We can move mountains but gravity will not make it easy to do, can we change gravity, not yet so again many things affect or guide the outcome of what we choose to do, many out of our control. Can we fly, yes, must we use a plane or other vehicle to do so, again yes. So no matter what we want we are limited in our options to achieve these objectives because we are driven by larger forces as of yet out of your control. I was told by a good friend the definition of a contract is that document the law can enforce, keep calm, keep it simple, truth should not be complicated, if it takes long paragraphs to explain perhaps it's not true; so it is with an explanation, usually the answer is right there in few words, too complicated listen closely!

We know the weather but still just speculate as to rain or shine, prepare for a birthday party outside and still we are at the mercy of nature. At best our science today can guess at what will occur and the average of success statistically is not good and our guess more often than not lands us wet although the forecast stated sunshine all day. Really loosen your grip on reality as your reality might not be the only one, all around you many different things affect it without our control so learn to go with the flow and much happier will we all become.

This is not to say we should stop going to school or learning for what are we if not the sum of all our parts so the better prepared we are for this uncertain world the better guess for our success in it with all the unknown variables around us. Sometimes one person's reality is another's crazy, how can we tell the difference, even if you stop believing, reality does not go away, so stay the course of your life find your reality and go with it. Success in any endeavor begins with knowing the destination, fix your gaze, remember great aim accomplishes great things, follow through with your plan, this concentrated energy will hit the mark; throw out discouragement, setbacks and keep on moving forwards as you go you will realize the journey and the pursuit of your goals are just as important as the final destination. Test your boundaries, realize they are paper thin and can be ripped through as soon as you realize they are but pit stops in the proses called growth!

Love is a powerful aphrodisiac, are you mature in your love; then if your love is there you would say I need you because I love you and not I love you because I need you. I can assume that when you feel loved by another you also gain strength, to go on, even in adverse circumstances, it must also be true then that we can become courageous and take more chances when we love someone deeply. With a loving heart life grows, it is not lack of love that makes unhappy marriages; it's our lack of acceptance because at some level we feel undeserving of this love. Always try and love unconditionally, remember true love only requires the happiness of our one true love, with this essential ingredient our own loving heart can soar. There is no bankruptcy in love, it's an endless supply, created and recreated, just when you think there is no more, you are spent, creation opens another door to love and to be loved, all it takes is an opportunity.

When you're loved and they speak your name it's different than all others because you just know they mean what they say and all that comes with your name in it. Dive into your relationship, don't waiver, don't doubt, don't let insecurity seep in. You could have been the love of her life you could have ruined her lipstick you could have rocked her world instead she chose to make you a memory. a love story that never was; so often this is true, choose to brave the unknown for this is your chance at happiness, it takes risk to open yourself but the rewards are worth it. In life we can either be spectators or participators, who you are; who you will become is still up to you. Make the right choice and let the love story be one that was.

Let's switch gear, when are we considered living, and or dead; what part does the soul play, how do we know the difference. All good questions, I've had the opportunity to work with some people who have had some catastrophic brain damage but still breathing. Some clients tell me they feel the person is still there while others simply feel bad about pulling the plug; some have asked me to make the determination if there is a soul yet in that body. Not all answers are the same, most of the time the soul goes when the body dies, but with today's advancement in science no one is sure. Ancient Egyptians believed it was in the heart and nothing to do with the brain as they even took the brain out through the nose as waste product while others believe that the brain is the housing for the soul.

One thing is for sure, a large percentage of this world believes in a soul and life after death, so why so negative about out of body experiences or near death out of body experiences. Its all the same thing, does not matter if we are able to detach or the soul is detached because of some sort of trauma, let's keep an open mind and allow yourself to belief what so many claim they have experienced. Look, science has proven that there is something there, something even if probes can't determine but it's there. Many claim to have had a moment soon after a loved one passed and they had no idea in some cases that was the case. So we are more connected at the spirit level than sometimes at the technological level. Many have learned at will to disconnect, I can channel by traveling my mind, remote viewing. I've done soul travel but found it to be less than practical and more dangerous as you leave yourself exposes to other forces.

There is an order in the universe, what I mean by this is when you are wearing old shoes in a dream for example and someone or some spirit replaces the with better ones for sure a good thing is coming for you. If for example it's an entire change of wardrobe it usually means a more life altering situation. I got a phone call from a good client who the previous night in a dream was wearing flip flops, she told me she usually wear that type of shoes for her day to day and in the dream she had someone take them off and replace them with high heal gold shoes with a streak of silver. I told her that something good was coming for her probably work related. She was so excited she got that vision because as she arrived to work that morning she was given a raise not only monetarily but position. If people pay attention to their dreams they will usually get messages randomly. We are always been looked after by the spirits assigned to us, unfortunately we are so filled with the day to day activities that let's face it all humans deal with.

The universe you will find with practice is on your side, the more we do nothing we are like a ship at sea with no direction it goes where the wind and waves takes it. Add a sail and you can guide it, add an engine and you can totally control its direction. Remember a sail might not be as quick but you will never run out of fuel nor will you make such rash choices that it will become impossible to stop in time so what I'm telling you tread lightly until you get good at what you are doing. We can all step on the gas and go faster and faster but there is a point we can lose control. Magic can be intoxicating, especially when we start to see results from our work but unfortunately there are dark forces out there that will temp us and attempt to misguide us.

Always work on the side of right on the side of light and God forgives ignorance, once you start doing malice for its own case we are in uncharted territory and there is a point of no return; my fondest wish is none who read this book will ever allow themselves to be romanced into that dark road. It's easy to go there because it does offer easy answers and easy pickings but like they say nothing is free and sooner or later you will be asked to pay the piper, unfortunately the payment can often be blood or life, the least if it's your own as this was your choice unfortunately a loved one can just as easily be the cost, an innocent could be the payment existed for your foolish decisions.

I've been involved in many situations where making the easy choice would have made me some serious money but if you ground in what I wrote above and realize when you make deals with the shades of life the price is often more than you are willing to pay. Unfortunately once you make your bargains it's hard to change the cost after the fact. I remember one time where a woman wanted a man, she paid a man to do a spell to break a marriage and allow her to possess yes possess because like she wanted it you can't really call it love. Well it seemed to work for her as in one year the couple divorced and she managed to get this man to marry her. You would think wow that is magic but she got pregnant and the child was to come out with spinal bifida. I was called within the early part of the pregnancy and I was able to negotiate for that soul so it was fixed while in the womb.

How many of you will have the knowledge to call someone like me, most that do what she did it's a onetime deal and they have no clue on how the universe works. If energy pushes in a direction it continues unless stopped or something pushes in the opposite direction. I feel most of the time with good energy we can help most situations if you catch it before the wave becomes so big it's impossible to stop. Prayer is a key element, always start by asking for things with prayer, often you will be shown what you need to do. Yes action on our part is often needed to achieve our goals.

Don't act so surprised, what do you think magic is, it will unlike what you believe not drop on your lap as if by magic you must move pieces like on a chess board for all to fall where you need it.

Again I will emphasize look at your goal whatever it is and make sure it's for the greater good and not just for your good and crush everyone and everything else that becomes an obstacle. Sounds reasonable but when you are in the soup sometimes it's difficult so this is why I ask pray for guidance before you attempt to execute a plan without looking at all the possibilities first. Don't let bitterness or negative people change you, if they say you've changed, is that a bad thing, or did they just realize you are no longer doing it their way; most unhappy people I know constantly worry about what others think!

*A friend showed me this mathematical equation, I was so in awe of if that I wanted to share this with my readers; most definitely "food 4 thought".

In the equation it was proven that anyone can give 101%, you say how can anything truly more than 100% of everything; here is what he showed me through mathematics.

He showed me the alphabet: A B C D E F G H I J K L M N O P Q R S T U V W X Y Z converted to equivalent numbers: 1, 2, 3, 4, 5, 6, 7, 8, 9, 10, 11, 12, 13, 14, 15, 16, 17, 18, 19, 20, 21, 22, 23, 24, 25, 26.

Then he gave me these key words to convert

H A R D   W O R K

8+1+18+4 + 23+15+18+11= 98%

AND

K N O W L E D G E

11+14+15+23+12+5+4+7+5 = 96%

AND

A T T I T U D E

1+20+20+9+20+21+4+5 = 100%

THEN IT IS LOGIC TO REACH 101% WE MUST ACCEPT THE FREELY GIVEN LOVE OF GOD

L O V E   O F G O D

12+15+22+5 + 15+6 + 7+15+4 = 101%

God is not religion, please understand there is a difference, religion is simply what humans have invented in attempts to answer what God is. So take with a grain of salt when you are being barraged by those so called religious zealots who proclaim theirs to be the one true religion or the one true path to God. Remember, God is all about free will for the spirit to learn; what are we, spirits with a very temporary body to exchange experiences and grow.

I think as long as what you believe in is for the greater good then why not, what I have a problem with is those who proclaim if you do not join their bandwagon to hell you will go. By hell I mean to be penalized in one way or another or the lack of belief in what they believe in. I say live and let live, how can we be so arrogant that ours is the word and all others are wrong. Look around at how many beliefs some organized religion others more like concepts or a way of living. So who is really to say the absolute truth belongs to one group or another.

This book is not about who's right or who's wrong more so about living a good life, a fulfilled life according to what makes you happy and with the possibility only the possibility that if you belief in God in your own way that is enough without the guidance of a book to tell you absolutely that theirs is the truth or to hell you will go. Use any and all guides to help you better understand our existence and take away from each the best without being bound to any dogma that unleashes pain and suffering if you deviate from the letter of their dogma.

Chapter 2
By The Numbers

Let's see the many ways we can improve our lives, day to day, spell to spell, magic to magic. What does it all mean; we can do things to improve our lives through spell work, what is spell work. In my opinion anyway we can use energy to help ourselves or others, there are some rules to follow for in life there are consequences to most things we do. One important one, always try and do the right thing by others as you would for yourself. I know there can be gray areas in everything we do and black and white can be an oversimplification to most day to day life decisions. So I will outline some examples I think might help guide your choices as you progress in this path of magic. If you would not be alright with someone doing the same thing to you then odds are with very few exceptions you should not do it to someone else. Free will is a biggie so once we infringe on the right to choose of another there can be some ramifications. The lash back if at all depends on the severity of the infringement. Let's face it in law when you steal 20 cent item you will most likely not be sent to the death penalty so it is with magical infringement. The limit as to what we can do is much like the talented athlete, the better the athlete the more he or she can accomplish in their field of endeavor. Like any other activity the more you practice the better you will get and there are of course those as in athletes that have natural abilities that make them seem like without effort they achieve. So are with some A students in academics, no study and still ace that final while others burn the midnight oil and get by with a B-.

There are more freedoms in cleaning than most other spell work, when we take a shower we get rid of odors and worse, so it is with cleansings. Some with but a prayer and done, others we actually need to bring in tools of the trade. These tools can vary from blood offerings as in animal sacrifice, fruits, plants, actual baths and many other items available to us. I prefer to start simply by offering the same food as we eat, placing it outside or at an altar of your own design; offer up a plate that would have otherwise been eaten in your home to share as a token of appreciation or belief. For example if we wish to have something manifest in our lives we can take a red apple and open the top with a knife and write on a brown paper bag with pencil our desire and fold it and place it back inside the apple. Adding a little honey, close the apple again, wrapping it in a red bow and placing it next to a royal palm tree. You may linger, lean on the tree, place hand on it and let it know what you have left there and what you asked for, in other words your intent.

Take several vases in the home and buy flowers for them, as you cut the stem and add to the vase express to the spirits of your home or where you are how those flowers are placed around the home as center pieces in gratitude for something you have asked for. State that if your wish is honored you would serve up another set of flowers around the home in gratitude. Although speaking out loud does not help any more than doing it as a quiet thought in your mind it does help as you know an idea will sometimes sound crazy after you say it out loud and not so much in your head.

The simplest magic is the prayer type so if you are a church goer try at least several times in a week for a month to stop off at a local church when no one is there, in other words when the preacher is not giving a sermon but the quiet of the church is in full swing. Then you may enter and sit, silently pray or out loud does not matter. Once you feel you have dispelled any doubt as to your resolve for your wish then you may leave. I've seen over the years many so called prayers come to fruition quickly so don't doubt they work. Leave it in God's hands seems to work for me the best. In other words I don't tell God what I want but instead that I'm in need and leave it in his hands as to how to find the solution. If romance don't say who you want in your life but rather ask God to provide what is best for you and you will accept his choice because as a wise and just God what he sends will be a blessing in your life and your future home.

In magic when we do something there is always a ripple effect, these days more than 50% of the spells I'm asked to do I simply pray on them and I can manifest the answer, so can you with practice and some of the tools I will offer in this book. Once we have harnessed the power of thought other steps to achievement will be much easier. Once you acquire the power of belief, you've seen it people with no education running big corporations and PHD's working for minimum wage, self-confidence grants your chances for success in any endeavor better than average. With self-confidence you will have more freedom to prepare for success, so don't overvalue what you lack and for goodness sake stop undervaluing who you are! Most of the time in life less is more, so prepare to give your message, preparation is everything, to speak nonsense just start any time but if you want to have impact and be successful preparation is key, keep your word for that will be your unbroken bond that all will trust!

Make visible what without you, might never have been seen, your words carry weight, create messages that inspire say what you mean and mean what you say, others will follow! In this world of magic the spoken word can have a physically manifested reality so once you acquire that power use it wisely as easy come easy go. You can easily lose all you have gained if you abuse your knowledge. There are always spirits to assist you and with time they can withdraw their support if it's felt you are abusing the gift. There are those that don't care and abuse is what they hope for. Hopefully you will not go that route because there are always consequences to abuse.

Let's talk of star or moon magic, on the night of the full moon you can get a pot and add water, some star anise, some honey, some cinnamon sticks, some sugar, I like by the seat of my pants magic; in other words do what you feel, I find that most spells written won't work exactly the same for someone else. So back to the spell, put the whole thing to boil, once it is boiling turn off the heat and let it cool. Grab a bottle of beer and pour it in the mix, then take three perfumes of your own use and spray a few times in the mix. Stick your hands in there and make sure it's well mixed up. While you have your hands in there pray to God and ask as you humbly prepare this energy bath allow it to endow you with that witch you request. Take it outside and at midnight face the full moon and as you grasp it with both hands raise it over head asking mother moon to give its energies and bless this bath so as to grant you your wish. It is at this moment that you ask for what you want. Lower it and do the same thing two more times and then go back inside and after you bathe grab the bath and pour it over your head. All you do is dry it off, some people are sensitive to certain ingredients for example my step son gets a rash with cinnamon so I modify his to have the desired effects and not the rash. Magic is trial and error, just do it with good intent and feeling so it will provide the desired effect. Never do magic while angry as you can just as easily bring along negative energies and you don't want to walk that route.

I had a young man come to me with a dilemma, he wanted into a specific program and although his grades would do, every time he attempted to take the exam to get into the program he would choke and fail miserably. He told me he knew the material but blanked out. I cleared his energies and gave him a bath he was to take the morning of the exam; I told him there is a no fail scenario if he truly knew his stuff. It was a couple of days later that I got a call, he was so happy from failing twice to acing the exam. He told me point blank he was focused and calm, just as I had told him he did great. Magic can enhance what is already supposed to happen, as in this case the bath simply allowed his best self to come through and accomplish what he was supposed to do.

Let's talk Rue, it's a plant you should be able to easily acquire. I like to get cheap cologne like baby violet or any big bottle with liquor content and not expensive. Open the bottle and it must have available to you a big enough opening to place the plant or some branches in there. Let it soak for a week or so and then on a regular basis after you bathe grab handfuls of the mix and apply to the back of the neck, the arm pits the back of the knee, rub on the shoulders and any other part you like. Oh, before I forget try and not use it if you had been sweating before as it can in some cases cause an allergic reaction with a sweaty skin. I've only experienced it while doing cleansings with the plant itself but just case. Below is a picture of the Rue plant.

When you want to clean a home you believe has negative or stagnant energy you may grind this plant in water; do it with your own hands, as you grind give it purpose, let it sit so it dissolves its juices and then mop the floor. If you want you may also place this plant under the bed until it dries completely, we never waste so after it's dry you may use it as incense by placing it in a small pot of some kind and adding some hot carbons like from a barbeque so it will burn as you walk your home to let the smoke cleanse the ambiance.

I love the plant kingdom and one of the best is Rompe Saraguey, you can find it in most warm climates. This plant has been said to have not only curative abilities for breaking negative energies but also to improve health. I can't tell you about health but I can tell you if you take it and break it up in a bucket and grind it down in the water, again always use your own hands to give it intent. Takes a couple of hours before use as to allow it's juices to truly be released into the bucket, then after a regular shower you may pour the entire contents over your head. If you are going to do it outside take all the leaves and grind on your body making emphasis on the arms and legs not forgetting the back of the neck, then pour the bucket over your head. Let it air dry for a bit before you dry off.

If you want to do indoors just strain the contents out of the bucket and pour the water over head after the shower and dry off. You should do this one for three consecutive days and sit back to reap the rewards; incredible to feel better and see it manifest all around you. When I do baths or any other sort of cleanse place your needs in God's hands and allow the energies to do their thing in the best direction for your good. There are many that guide the cleansings to what they wish so you may do that as well; as you pour ask for what you want to happen. Always keep in mind the universe knows long distance much better than us what each of us needs and this does not always match with what we want.

Rompe Saraguey may also be used to cleanse the person by binding together several branches, wetting them with perfume, alcohol or liquor and running over the entire body of the person as they stand in front of you. You can take the branches and hit the person all over from head to toe, ask them to lean on something and hit the bottoms of their feet as well. Once done you may place the branches on the floor and ask the person to stomp or clean their feet over the plant to make sure they clear their path. Then you can add alcohol over the plant and set it on fire, always using care not to set a fire anywhere else by accident. Many religions including Santeria use this plant and if you research over the internet I'm sure you will find other remedies used for this very popular plant.

I like to get in shorts and in the back yard start grabbing the ground plant from the bucket and starting with the back of the head, neck areas start to friction. Work your way down to chest area, stomach, low back, continue until you use most of the shredded plant in the bucket; remember always finish with your legs and feet area. As you do this part of the cleaning ask for all that does not belong in your aura to be gone and then once you are done with the herb part take the bucket and pour over your head so it flows throughout your body. Don't dry off just let it dry while it's on your body, so if you are in a cold climate you may just strain the bath free of the herb and in this case divide it into two parts and once you shower pour it over head and just dry off. On the following day do the same the same with the remainder of the bath. <u>The following picture of a Rompe Saraguey plant.</u>

I must remind you that my recipes are mine and once you begin to communicate with your spirits they will no doubt give you what they consider best for you. These are generic recipes that will work no matter but fine tuning is always preferred. So for example when a person calls me for a reading I will ask for the birthday and according to their energies I will give them a mixture that will be especially suited for them and for their energy needs according to the stars that are favorable to them.

Now I would like to talk about the Ceiba Tree, it's considered sacred by many people and religions to include the great Maya civilization. It's believed to be the tree in its totality to connect heaven to earth and all the realms in between. You may do an endless about of ritual with this tree. I will give you some basic ones but I believe once you get a feel for it you might want to plant one of your own. In some parts of the world, especially the rain forest type places this mighty tree can tower over the rest as its trunk can exceed 8 feet in diameter when fully grown.

Like most plants I use the Ceiba can be used to clear out spaces that might have negative energy. You can get some branches and pour some alcohol on it and walk the place to be cleared waving or spinning the branches like a whirlwind overhead and in the directions to be cleared like corners and open doorways. I like using seven branches in a bunch but it's really taste rather than ritual so you may use anywhere from three branches clumped up and or more to do this type of clearing. Again you may also use these bunches much the same to clear a person's energies, just remember when you pass the branches over the person be careful with the eyes and not to hit them too hard. Unless you're mad at them and want to get back like a client told me while I was doing a house clearing. The son told me to hit the mother hard until she was a pain, you know kids no matter the situation they will find a way to get the upper hand.

If you decide to get the plant make sure you use a very large clearing area in your yard, my own plant has grown over 50 feet in less than 4 years. Upon opening the hole you should speak to the plant and explain how it's to become part of your family and as you care for it and it grows may your abundance grow for all in the home. Explain how through the use of its leaves in all the different ways it may maintain the health of the people it helps. Not only physical health but spiritual health try and communicate with it often. Place your hands on the trunk and tell it as you water it how important it is in your home and how as it grows it will help grow the health of the land and you promise to water it and care for it so in return it will do the same for all you ask it. I recommend waiting at the very least six months before you start using its branches, remember it's a living thing and must also bind with you. This goes for most plants you use from your own home. Before you start asking a friend or before a friendship becomes strong it takes one thing, time so it is with plants or trees, nature in general.

When I need plants that I do not have off to the forest I go, some plants are around your neighborhood so scout the area. Once you know where most of the plants you will use regularly are located it becomes habit to go straight to it. I like to talk to my plants at least briefly, for example when I look for plants other than those I care for in my yard I like to offer up three pennies to the ground around where they are growing. I do this to acknowledge that I'm taking a small part of them and I usually tell them the purpose all before I pull one leaf. Once you find your patch or area to pull or cut from a relationship is created and you don't have to do this every time. Just a quick thank you for always giving the best you got to do the best for others is enough.

When you start making baths you will find the leaves are kind of gooey so don't worry as this is what the plant lets out as you grind it. Like I stated before it's one of the most religious plants as many peoples pray to it and use it in rituals, they believe that all spirits and saints are residing within the tree and it's a venue to communicate with them through the tree. Some even call Ceiba the tree of life for its ancient origins and it's scattered throughout the planet. It towers above in a canopy type spread and flowers once a year and in some areas may skip several years. The flowers I like to use as perfumes, I take cheap large bottles like violet for children, empty some out and fill with the flowers of the Ceiba tree. Within weeks the leaves will release its energy into this perfume and you may use it on a regular basis to keep your energies clean. Interestingly enough if there are bats in your area the flowers may attract them but don't fear it blooms only for a couple of months out of the year. You can take the branches and place them under your bed as they dry they will scatter all negative energies from your sleeping area. Once the branches are dry make sure in a safe way to prevent fires you burn them; I place them inside a metal drum and light it on fire with some alcohol. Stay in the area to make sure no embers escape and set a fire but also the smoke has cleansing capabilities.

IF your tree begins to bear the silky cotton, do not discard them as they may prove to be the most powerful part of the tree, remember this tree can grow under the right environment 200 plus feet and can in some areas exceed 8 feet in diameter. This silky cotton can be used in rituals, so let's look at one in detail. Get the cotton and save it until you have enough to place over a person's head. Open up a coconut and take the white pulp out, place it in your mouth and grind with your teeth. Use some coconut pulp, the natural stuff not medicated or with other ingredients and mix it in with the cotton and add that ground up coconut pulp.

This entire mix may be used in the affected area for example for someone who is having mental issues or tormented you may place it over their heads and add a little cap to keep it in place for at least an hour. The longer the better, so if you can simply watch TV while it's there even better. Once it's done you may remove it and simply throw it away and take a shower to remove the stuff left in the hair. I you don't have or can't get the cotton from the Ceiba you may use regular cotton as it will work as well. If you have access to a cotton tree you may use its leaves as a bath, much like I've described before but at the time where you are going to do it, use the ground up leaves and scrub your head with them as it has calming properties. This bath like the rest, just pour overhead and dry off.

No matter the plant ritual, no matter the plant I say waste not, so with this in mind as you use the branches or leaves let them dry and after they are truly dried out make a fire with carbon like a barbecue and place them over the burning embers of carbon, as the plant burns it's smoke can be used as a natural cleanse. For example you may cross over the fire as the smoke is released, over and over, back and forth so as it rises over your body it will further cleanse your energies and your aura may be totally clear from any negative energy. Remember waste nothing in nature, there is a purpose for all. <u>The following picture is of my own Ceiba tree</u>, it's only four years old and I've already had to cut down branches three times. It got to over fifty feet and that is just too big for my yard. If you notice the little house under it is where I clean the people that come to me for cleansings. If you observe above it is the only area of the entire plant with the flowers, giving me blessings for what I'm doing.

Here's one that I like for its refreshing qualities, siempre viva plant is not very big so you may plant it almost anywhere and it will flourish. Some attribute many curative powers; I like how in bath form it refreshes all the body's general energy. For example just fill your bucket with water and add some of the leaves and crush with your hands. Don't change your routine as you are crunching the plant in the bucket full of water pray and pray some more ask the universe to use all the powers of this plant to heal and save our energies from any harm. You may also grab one leaf and place it in a swollen area or an area with any form of physical injuries and wrap it with a damp cloth. If it works you should see the results within a couple of hours; as I told you I prefer using it as a general bath but if you check on line you will find many have great faith in this plant. If you look below there are two different varieties of Siempre viva, like these there are in the plant kingdom several types of the same plant so if you use them you might find one works better for you. The one on the left blooms a beautiful bush of yellow flowers during the winter months and the one on the right just a little purple looking bulb sporadically throughout the year. I like the one on the top during the time it blooms as it seems to have more energy and the one on the bottom I use throughout the year.

Most plant baths are very similar, some folks like to boil the plant and then strain out the residual and just use the water. I think we can use all parts of the plant, so scrubbing the plant on your body before you pour the water mixture is good. Allowing that plant you scrubbed to dry out and then lighting on fire is also a good one. Bottom line in my opinion we should not boil the plant in water to get its juices out because you may lose some of not most of its curative abilities in the boiling. I think as I've described before in most of the baths I've outlined previously you should place the plants in water grind with your own hands and as you do ask God to allow these natural juices to fulfill their purpose and help you in whatever endeavors and reasons you have for using them. Remember always have a reason if that reason is just to ask the universe to give energy to this bath for whatever is best for you and not for a targeted result.

We all carry our own set of rules along with the spirits that work with us so trust your feelings and use what I give you as a general guide. For example, I gave my favorite cleansing to one of my clients while on a phone reading. They were to shower, stay wet and use salt to scrub or defoliate their entire body from neck on down, wash it off then repeat using sugar. I usually like this cleanse to be repeated three days straight but I prefer it be done just before bed. For this client on the first day she did not get much from it but on the second she tried it first thing in the morning and she had the best day in months so she called and I told her to follow her feelings and try the third in the morning and as she did the same results wonderful. She called me back and I agreed she should repeat that first cleaning again and do it in the morning and she did. Soon after she got the benefits but from a morning cleanse not evening. Her star was the sun and not an evening one so who new, I'm not strict about much because who I'm I to say it must be so. If it works that is the best gauge for success, not the rule but the exception some times.

The creation of reality can be manifest with tools like plants, take the Jericho flower, you can order it on the web from different sites. This plant comes dry and if you get a glass bowl fill with water add the plant and say your request. For example if you wish to put back on the right path your love life with your partner you may say as this flower blooms, as this plant replenishes, may our love be rekindled, as this flower gives children may our love be renewed. As an example, it can be used to eliminate obstacles so place the bowl up high and ask as this spell blooms as this flower flourishes and regrows so may my business flourish and as it gives birth to children so may our love give birth to a child. You get the idea take care of the plant and it will take care of you.

Caisimon is another plant in my repertoire that has many uses. It's easy to plant; even from a leaf you can grow a plant. You can use its leaves to boil into a tea to ease stomach issues. You may grind in a bath to pour overhead and promote positive energy. You can even use it to place it on an area of the body that is not right, for example you may have feet that are hurting. I that case you may take the shoe off and the sox and then place the plant on the bottom of your foot and put the sox back and the shoe. You can do this with most body parts, remember use it and then take it off after a while and keep on using it as long as needed. Most of the time if it's going to work it will within hours and not days.

You have a desire to improve your health or the health of a loved one you may use this same plant for that reason. Ask for the healing powers of the universe to descend upon that person and as the flower blooms so may their health have a quick recovery. As the green return to its leaves may health return to the person's life. Use your own words remember what ever seems natural to you will impact in the universe the best. You always want to use spell magic with resolve, have no doubt and it will have the greatest impact. The following picture is of Caisimon.

Papaya tree also has many curative properties, you can use the papaya itself or one of my favorites is the leaf. You may get them from the tree and wet them with fresh water, then you can scrub your scalp with them for a good amount of time for example you may take five to seven leaves and after you wet them you can scrub your own scalp or the scalp of another until your hands feel hot. Remember when you do these things try and be in a good mental place, do your prayers first and once you feel in the zone you can start. Rub and rub some more until it actually starts to break, but if you can stay with it until you feel the heat from the plant and or from your hands. It has the ability to refresh the thought proses so if someone is stressed out it's a no brainer to cool your melon or someone else's so the thoughts are not so amped up.

Everyone is open to negative energy, the other day I went to clean an elderly couple who had never been cleaned energy wise before. That evening I cleaned myself with a cigar, and wow it was all over the place. That following week the clients that called for appointments were cut in half. I cleaned myself several times and with each consecutive day the cigar was better until perfectly round. Remember I clean with cigar as a thermometer of the surrounding energy of the person and speaks to me. So with this example I show how all including me can be affected by negative energy even if no bad spirits are around. Remember we live in a fluid world, so just as we can at any time catch a cold we can have negative energy attaching to us. The goal is not to let it get worse with time. A simple cold can end up with pneumonia if not cared for; remember if you visit a doctor with a bad cold he could give you an antibiotic injection but will usually follow it with a cycle of antibiotic pills. So using the same reasoning I send most baths for three days to make sure to completely get rid of the sour energy that might be around.

One of the strongest trees for disarming the negative energy from dark forces is Pomarosa; this tree usually grows close to water, fresh water that is. It's big so don't go planting it in a small garden. It can grow very large if left to run wild so find an area that would fit a plant that can do upwards of 30 feet or more. I like its attributes because there is no one part of this tree that is not used for work in the spiritual realm. Most that know its power will plant one in front of their home; it has the power to disarm all that come to do bad to your home. I've seen a dark magic practitioner get close to the plant and start to feel uncomfortable to the point that he had to leave the area.

You can use its leaves to grind in a bucket of water and leave it for a while before you pour over head. You can use its branches to clear an area of negative energies or just plain stagnant energies. Just grab a few branches and bind together with a red rag, pour some alcohol on them and swing over head or at corners in every room in your home. Once you are done take the plant out back and pour more alcohol then light it on fire to disperse all that it has picked up while you were cleaning. You can place branches under the bed and leave them there till they dry, again take out back pour alcohol and light on fire to dispel all it might have absorbed. Even the seeds are useful, for example in a place where a dark magic practitioner works you can grind the seeds to a powder and sprinkle it and all the energies that aid that person will at least temporarily disperse. If you want an area protected, you may grind the seeds and sprinkle in that area and as long as the powder is there no negative strength can be gathered there. In other words negative energy can exist but it won't have any power to do harm in that area. It's so powerful that some say as a bath no one person should do it more than two or three times in a year. I say if you need it use it, so what is the use of having this cure if you're afraid of doing it; remember most medicine has probable side effects but it's better to take out the problem, same with this plant. Find below a picture of the Pomarosa plant, I had just cut these to do the house cleanse for a client!

Abre Camino is another very handy plant, as the name implies in Spanish it opens roads and as a bonus smells great. I have several on both side of my front door and when there is no wind and the odor permits you can walk in and as you do smell its wonderful fragrance. It's a plant that is used in many magical spells, some use it as a solitary plant others add it to their mix. Keep in mind how good it smells so as a bath it's great so you can do it after your shower then pour it over head and simply dry off. When I do it no cologne is necessary, when I do it for my wife her coworkers then her how good she smells and inquire about the perfume. It's a great plant to bring good things to you in a bath form. I also like to get the branches and add a little perfume and swing it around as I walk my home to keep the energies flowing, when you do this no stagnant energy will stay and the flow of the home gets better. You may even create magical amulets of protection with it; the uses are endless and since it's a plant that mixes well with others the spells and baths are endless. So as part of a heavy cleaning I would use this plant as desert, I mean use the heave duty stuff to clear the area or person then this one to refresh as it's not particularly strong but it's strength is in its ability to generate positive flow.

I like spells that are for self and not infringing on the free will of others but that's me, you may have talents that make those more difficult spells work as if by magic. I still caution doing things against the will of others although there are exceptions to any rule. Sage other than the traditional culinary use can and is used for many reasons one that should not be undervalued is its use to promote contractions in women and or also contractions for pregnant women. I prefer to use it in my cleansing rituals in baths or the plant itself to swing it in a home to clear negativity from the ambiance.

In a similar type of cleaning you may use another type of plant to fill your hands with, not really sure, just use some from your own back yard. Add perfume but this time get some charcoal and light it on fire inside a deep pot so it will not spill to ground and burn the grass or where ever you are doing this. Once the coals are hot you may pass the plant in your hand over the heated coals and pass them by the body of the person you are cleaning, add church incense or any other available incense to the coals to create smoke that as you pass the plants over them they will amplify the power of the plant and the smoke with come along on the plants ride to the person further amplifying its cleaning powers. After you are done place the plants over the hot coals so it will burn them, again pass over them three times and walk away.

Boton de oro is a marvelous plant that can cleanse your aura, your home or even bring love to your life. Its energy is said if used frequently can attract what you want to your life, so I say be careful what you wish for. Like all the other plants I've spoken about it can be used in any of these ways. It has a little yellow flower and you may use this plant for cleansing and spells alike. Its biggest attribute in my opinion is its attraction qualities when used in bath form. If you want to be liked more or bring a partner into your life, this is the bath to do. If you want to be seen because you feel people are just not paying attention to you again this is the plant. It can grow big so be careful where you plant this robust plant.

No matter how you evolve spiritually a large portion of this knowledge will include plants and its uses. Remember the more you know the more you can help yourself and others, so with knowledge comes power and responsibility for its use. Innocence is forgiven but not when you use or misuse your knowledge for gain without care to consequences for others. Keep this simple mantra "do good to all with harm to none" and you should stay on the path.

I like spells that are for self and not infringing on the free will of others but that's me, you may have talents that make those more difficult spells work as if by magic. I still caution doing things against the will of others although there are exceptions. If you have a desire to improve your health or the health of a loved one you may use this same plant for that reason. Ask for the healing powers of the universe to descend upon that person and as the flower blooms so may their health have a quick recovery. As the green return to its leaves may health return to the person's life. Use your own words remember what ever seems natural to you will impact in the universe the best. You always want to use spell magic with resolve, have no doubt and it will have the greatest impact.

In magic nothing is wasted, let's say you used some plants to clean a person's energies, for example grab some fresh sage and hold it in your right hand, add perfume or cologne; maybe just alcohol will do the trick. Some will use liquor, the power ingredient is not as important as it is to use something if nothing is available just fresh water will do. So you whack the person from head to toe, beating them with the plant and asking it to dispel any negative energy they might be holding on to or to detach a negative spirit that might be causing turbulence in the person's life. Once done you can throw the plant to the ground and ask the person who was just cleaned to stomp on this as if wiping their feet with hit. Immediately add alcohol or other combustible and light on fire; you and the person may now cross over the fire back and forth at least three times then walk away without looking back.

In a similar type of cleaning you may use another type of plant to fill your hands with, not really sure just use some from your own back yard. Add perfume but this time get some charcoal and light it on fire inside a deep pot so it will not spill to ground and burn the grass or where ever you are doing this. Once the coals are hot you may pass the plant in your hand over the heated coals and pass them by the body of the person you are cleaning, add church incense or any other available incense to the coals to create smoke that as you pass the plants over them they will amplify the power of the plant and the smoke with come along on the plants ride to the person further amplifying its cleaning powers. After you are done place the plants over the hot coals so it will burn them, again pass over them three times and walk away.

Live life to the fullest and leave a legacy your ancestors will be proud of, become a warrior for God, a warrior for good and the blood line you leave behind will reap the rewards of your good work. It's said we carry the actions of our ancestors with us, leave them good karma and as you pass on your soul will rejoice in all the good you have done, so will those you have left behind. Abundance creation can be as easy as belief, it's often easier to manifest through a totem. A totem is nothing more than a tool a talisman of sorts to channel what you are asking for. It's true we can often harness more power using a talisman than through thought alone. True enough we need nothing to manifest reality but if you can't focus and by you I mean most of us then by all means use one.

A simple one is a bowl where you would add let's say the picture of the person you wish to influence, make it in the form of a black and white photo copy add with pencil the persons full name three times over the picture. Place the picture in the bowl, add honey multi-color sprinkles; over that some brown sugar and elevate the spell over your head. I like to do this outdoors but anywhere will do, ask for your wish to unite in loves embrace with this other person stating their name, later you will add your own picture same as theirs face down over the other picture. Add more honey and powdered cinnamon again more honey then raise it up again and say as I unite us in this bowl may our to paths unite in a bond filled with passion and love. As you enter a position of trust and power, let go of the past, be slave to it no longer, grow the shroud of self-respect and remember once you invoke the power of love the world will know you as a patient man, a man with timing. Again these examples can be done in your own words and with feeling. You may use the spells you lift overhead at noon for the sun or for most power on the night of the full moon and at midnight!

The power of creation is in all living things so igniting that power in spell magic is an essential ingredient for success. So with that being said, you can find the egg shells from eggs that have hatched then you may crunch them up into a fine powder and use it to add a pinch to most if not all the spells of growth. For example find eggs from nests you know have hatched chicken eggs that have for sure hatched chicks. The key to this is only eggs that have hatched, you may even use eggs like from alligators, turtles etc. You may use them all together when you make your fine powder. On occasion I've even added dried lizard eggs, the key ingredient is they must have hatched else they are no good.

All living things have the power of creation so you may use feathers from animals to use spell magic, for example I've used condor feathers to add power to a cleaning, I had a smudge stick in one hand and as I blew on it to smudge the area of the person being cleaned and the home I was walking through I would use the condor feathers to further amplify my own power to clean the area. You may also use them to pick up some of the smoke and pass them around the body of the person being cleaned. I used condor feathers but any feathers will do, the concept of living things is a very powerful one; does not matter that the animal is not there the feathers will work nicely.

For example if you use a dove for cleaning you may find that a white one works a bit better but any dove has the power to detach negative energy or even an attachment; a negative spirit from another person or area. So grab it by the legs and move it up and down around the person or area so it flaps its wings it will clear all turbulent energies. Once you are done you may release the animal to fly away. There have been circumstances where what the animal picked up was great and it will just flop to the ground until it regains enough strength to fly again. This can take from a few minutes to a few days, never fear it will regain and fly away but the clearing would have been done and the person will feel better.

Smoke is a natural cleanser, so if you burn incense always move it around your body asking for all turbulent or negative energy be released into the universe and your own energies assert themselves. It's easy to pick up negative energies and with time if a healing or cleaning is not performed this energy can eventually cause blocks in your path of life; so regular energy work should be performed as part of your life. Think about it, how often have you seen someone who looks scruffy but this person always dressed well, these cycles can go on and on until the low energy attachment is released. In your own life some days you feel terrible without a cause. You step into the shower and feel great after wards. Yea dirt of another kind can also make you feel down so that type of cleaning is also a good thing. Let's face it if you do not shower everyday bad energy is the least of your problems people would not want to be close to you for the odor. So it is at a more subtle level with energy; if you keep all your parts at a good level your chances to succeed will increase. Listen there is nothing guaranteed but if you can better your chances is it not worth the work.

To pray for another is another way to clean energy, if you infuse your thoughts with love or any other powerful positive thought energy, it will reach and the person will soon feel better. Try it and see, depending on how focused you are, is now soon you will begin to see results so meditation is key. The better you are in focusing and not allowing stray thoughts to interfere the better the result or at the very least the quicker. Give it a try, I believe therefore I will achieve. It's almost like creating a dejavu moment to create or manifest that reality. You know those moments that you've felt like you've been there or done that before, exactly but in reverse you are creating that moment ahead of time. The biggest seeds to abundance is created through gratitude, be grateful for all you have and grow it from there, that place, that fountain of abundance you already bring with you is the best place to grow your future from; let it grow let it grow let it flow! There is no expiration date to desire, you open the bottle and it only ends when you give up.

There is something called the four winds, whom ever is born under this sign will have a very tumultuous life. No matter the direction, no matter how well all seems, at the most inappropriate moment their life will turn on its head. So for those folks as I call them usually old souls come with lots of karma from previous lives need a simple ritual to free themselves of this. Let's say not free as we all have a little of this but a more manageable level. First you get 4 coconuts the ones they sell in the super-markets will do, take all the little hairs off them and paint them with chalk of different colors, I like as a general rule white, black, blue, green. There are exceptions where the spirit will give me a different color but for the most part those are the colors. Once painted on a flat surface you will paint four arrows to represent the four cardinal positions. North, South, East, West, making sure you have at the center enough room for a person and some room to wiggle so let's give it five feet away from north to south and east to west. With this space you may stand in the middle with the four arrows pointing away from you in the above mentioned directions. Please, look at the drawing below of the design I would ask you to do and draw the arrows facing away from the center and over the letters place each of the above described coconuts; don't forget when you buy them to shake them vigorously to reassure yourself they have water otherwise it will not work.

```
                    N



W                person                E



                    S
```

You may mark each arrow at the tail end with N, S, E, W; we want to make sure to pray to each of the correct winds. Now go back to the coconuts and place each one over the point part of the arrow or the letter representing the direction. Place some honey over each one, a little bread or equivalent cracker, some nuts, rice, corn and a sweet liquor of your choosing. Once a little of each of these ingredients were sprinkled over each of the coconuts you may then take a dozen incense sticks and light them all. Start facing north and summon the north wind, as you pass these lit sticks over your body blow on them in the northern direction summon the north wind to come and open your path of life in its direction. Then the same of the other cardinal positions going counter clockwise. Once you are back to north if the sticks are still smoking place all of them on the floor in front of the north facing arrow. Step back to the center and pick up that coconut over the north arrow. Say I summon the spirit of the north, may the north wind always lead me in the right direction, may the northern lights always light my way, and you do this while holding the coconut over your heart. Then lift over your head and shake it violently asking as you do this that all obstacles be gone and as you break this coconut may the north wind carry your wishes and your destiny forwards. Ask as you continue to shake the coconut overhead what you want in your life.

When you are done crush it with all your force over the arrow that faces north. The goal is as it shatters all or more than half of the pieces face or break facing with the white or inside part facing up. _You will do this counterclockwise to the remaining directions, one key element when you get the coconuts shake them assuring they have water in them, this is one of the essential ingredients for this spell. Once done and you observed how they broke pick up all the coconuts and add 21 pennies to the bag you got them in and drive to a street with four corner, park on one of the sides then leave it there.

Want to clean yourself or others without the expense of hiring someone, try simple household items like hydrogen peroxide. Fill a tub of water add a big bottle of this magic liquid and stay there at least 15 minutes then dry off. Still fill like it's not good enough or need something quicker, just take an empty gallon of milk or other container then add a glass full of baking soda, again take your normal shower and at the end pour over head then dry off. Even worse and need more then take a gallon of apple cider vinegar and just before you shower pour it over head while already in the shower and with no clothing. Wait a minute or two then begin your normal shower, always remember these are emergency formulas and it's always better to do the full treatments when possible, remember the tried and true salt and sugar scrub, this is another great home remedy just take your normal shower, immediately after while wet scrub your body with normal salt you have at home; that's right defoliate from the neck down to the toes to the fingertips then wash off, immediately do again but with sugar wash off with water again then dry.

Like I said, there are quickies for emergencies that will do the trick, if you have a need just get some champagne or sparkling water of some kind, like the sparkling nonalcoholic apple sider. As soon as you get into the tub before you shower pour over head, or you may do after you showers in either case over head and let it run down body. If you do after remember in the morning to do again as your body might stay sticky overnight. All above as showers may be done in tub baths as well. If you are in a funk, just grab your gallon of milk from the refrigerator and before you shower pour the entire contents of milk overhead from the container and as it comes down all over your body ask for clarity, freshness of mind and body, may this milk clear up your aura and bring you peace. Immediately after it's all over your body you may take your normal shower and shampoo of hair.

Many of us have issues with sleep, there are many reasons so I'll start with a simple cure, just take a plain glass of water, fill it with ice ¾ of the way then add salt, enough so the entire top of the ice is covered. Take this cup and place it under your bed close to where your head would rest as you sleep. Some people like to place it on the night stand closest to your head. Either way will work but how about if you decide you want to drink water that night, not fun. This should cool down any negative energy that might creep up on you as you sleep.

There are lots of snake charms to pass around all you need is the one that will work for the right situation, this is why people try things in books and they don't work. Like any antibiotic, if you do not have the right one for the right situation it will be a waste of medicine. Unlike aspirin or any over the counter type medication, its general like a broad spectrum antibiotic, it will do something just not exact so it might alleviate the symptoms but not necessarily cure the ill. That's why I recommend going to someone who is practiced in doing energy work; you won't go to someone with limited knowledge for surgery, so it is with this type of work. You can experiment and you might get lucky but you might also make it worse, so my suggestion is find someone reputable in your area and go with a professional.

There are all kinds of natural alternatives to get your system into good shape, for what you ask, I say quality of life is most important so keeping all things in the body running well is very important. Take sublingual vitamin B-12; say three times a day breakfast lunch and dinner, you can take more no problem say five a day if you wish. In either case spread out throughout the day will do. If you have a means to take it in injection form even better, you may do butt injections of 1cc or use the same little needles as diabetics filled it will equal to one cc so either way will work. There is an oil or pill from the black seed oil you can take either the pill or the oil, if the oil five drops with some honey should be plenty per day, great for many brain benefits such as better attention or focus. I like a pill that has three ingredients, calcium, magnesium, zinc, this trio can do wonders for the body so take it again three times a day, one each time to keep things humming.

Some I've spoken to have also found the pill to diminish their headaches by as much as 50%. If you want to buy peppermint oil and upon onset of the headache rub on both temples and the base of the skull and within 10 minutes you should notice the alleviation of the headache. A snack food that I recommend to keep everyone running is nuts, what type, hey I say go nuts with it, if you like it eat it, if you don't learn to like them. It's the super food as far as I'm concerned and you can get so many benefits even to quench that snack time hunger and hold down the fort against gaining weight. I'm sorry if I tend to repeat some things but it's so important it's worth the bore of reading it twice, take my hint and focus on it!

I don't want to harp on exercise as you hear on it all the time but three times a week of cardio, don't care where it comes from, spinning, walking, or any other form of cardiovascular is a must. I had a client who was doing all the modalities except exercise; he came to me with erection problems. As I was cleaning his energies I could see how depleted he was, he looked good but his energy was horrible. After he started all the above, without missing a beat within 30 days he called me and told me how happy his wife was and she would soon call me for a reading. He said not only was the problem gone but he had stamina to give her all the time she needed to get her own groove on. I was very happy and confirmations are always well received so if you are reading this thanks. If you have another validation no matter what the reason please email me as this is my proof that I'm on the right track. I'm given information to pass on but more often than that people don't follow up to tell me so please do.

Give yourself the treatment, avocado, grind soft avocado and coat your hair with it, add some olive oil to the mix, put a cap or not just have it on for at least one hour, great for many things including refreshing you thought proses. Skin issues, plop some honey on the area, some even use it as an antibiotic. I've heard many people talk about marijuana use, I'm on the fence, if it was legal I guess I might try it. I know for young people it does slow the desire centers, in other words if you are a regular user I've seen an a student go down to a c student in less than a year with regular use. Many more people die from drug "prescription" use than any marijuana user; as a matter of fact I have not heard of any marijuana users having died, I'm sure you might find some on the web. Like anything else pros and cons, if you are in bad pain and the doctor suggests it for this or any medicinal purpose who I'm I to say no. Raw food verses cooked food, yes some enzymes and other nutrients are killed during the cooking proses but raw food can be dangerous if not well kept.

Chakras

It's a body holistic process, you are what you eat but you are also what you think so keeping the mind in tip top shape will help keep the whole package running smoothly. Once you learn that the energy flow of the body is important you may look into for example acupuncture to activate flow. Most say there are seven chakras I like to say 9, as you know in martial arts they discuss the energy building zone, build your inner energy to overpower your opponent this is your first chakra. The second is in the pelvic area and sexuality and feelings area so if you have emotional issues this might be the first chakra to work on. The third gives you your confidence, it's a little bit above your belly button, if having digestive issues work on this chakra. The fourth is your compassion or heart, keep this one working well and your circulatory system will heal. Keep number five glowing if you deal with people, specially sales or just having to speak out to others this is your key chakra. Number six is the opening to the universe with it you can see and send out messages spiritually speaking. Number seven is the one you will use when meditating, so if you maintain this one open and healthy your whole system will glow. The 8th will be your shield, this is your bubble, surround yourself with number eight and nothing will harm you. Number nine is the one I use to travel, in time and space; there is nothing you can't do if your ninth chakra is working and healthy.

The Root Chakra is at the base of the spine, you would call it your tail bone area and usually associated with emotional issues; as the name implies it keeps you grounded. So those with low back pain should look into this chakra and open it up.

The Sacral Chakra is your lower abdomen more or less two inches below your naval also deals with emotional issues. If you're having sexual issues this is the one I would look to opening, also for people with fertility issues.

The solar plexus Chakra upper stomach area also houses emotional components that deal more with self-type stuff. If digestive problems or liver type issues this is where to look at as far as opening up this channel.

The Heart Chakra Is the love chakra and will manifest right over the heart area so if you're having circulatory problems or issues with the lungs go no further and open this chakra up. Mind you as I've said before in this book, always consult your doctor for any medical concerns. These suggestions should be looked at additionally to medical help only and not in lieu of.

The Throat Chakra, you guess correct if you think it has to do with communication and is in the throat area. I would also look into this chakra if you seem to be having problems with your immune system.

The third eye Chakra is the one that allows us to view the big picture; its bull's eye is right between your eyes. If you were going to use acupuncture there I call it the happy point as it also alleviates being overwhelmed. If we analyze the reasoning it could mean the chakra is open more than your soul can manage so that point levels the aperture so your soul can better manage all the impute. So with this being said if there are any neurological deficiencies this would be the area to investigate.

The crown Chakra, some say is the highest point, the point that fully connects us to our spiritual side. As you can see above there are in fact two more above it that allow us to navigate better through this and the other realms. If spiritually disconnected, I would try opening this point to the universe and reconnect with your soul.

Remember how important exercise is, when you are warming up always stretch and when cooling down walk and stretch no matter the exercise. If you are a thinker or floater as I like to call them; that means you go off as your mind wonders from the task I do a kind of O.C.D. thing but it works; count three to five steps and make this work with your breathing. Say you take a breath to your three to five steps then equivalently exhale to another three to five steps until you get your mind back on the task at hand. If you drink and need quick fix naturally drink plenty of fluids to flush the toxins and stretch to help those toxins from your joints. I know that when you drink too much from experience ache is one of the problems so do some yoga, any form of stretching all the joints and making you limber will go a long way in helping all the water you are taking to take out the toxins from your body.

No matter what you do in life there are certain things you must follow in order to have order in your world, if your body is not healthy then there is a problem. The same with the mind so keeping it as a well-oiled machine is important. Many of us workout but neglect our emotions, having balance is important, it's not about any one thing, remember bottled up emotions can bring the body crumbling with disease. So as we grow and help our children to grow we must keep in mind that the whole is more important than any one part, divide equal time to keep this life balanced and healthy, remember the quality of life is just as important if not more so than the quantity of years. Look, we all have handicaps and jealousy and envy can be a negative way to proses these emotions. Take a step back, if you find a close friend or family member suddenly succeeds its normal to be out of sorts, but if you consider approaching the person and congratulating them and asking how they accomplished, then looking inward at your own triumphs and what steps to achieve on your own design you will forever have learned to move forwards to eventual success.

Chapter 3
Stories

20 year forecast

Some situations are so weird we have to scratch our heads just to wrap them around them. So it was in this reading, a woman called me referred by a client as are over 90% of my readings. She just listened as I began my reading, unlike most readings I began by telling her she had a choice to make, something from her past had come back to haunt her. She opened up by telling me another medium had told her many years ago that something would happen to her in the future that could potentially destroy her life. She told me that forecast of over 20 years prior had just come to pass and she needed clarity. I told her that something's are unfortunately doomed to pass. She then told me what had happened so many years ago that had come back to bite her. She explained that she had gotten married 25 years ago and early on things were a bit difficult in the relationship. She traveled for her job at the time and in one of those trips she was unfaithful to her husband, not an affair just a one night stand, a mistake as she calls it. Never again had anything happened and she had spent the following 20 years making amends by becoming a good wife and mother. She told me her marriage was wonderful and he was a wonderful husband. She than told me of the problem, that one night stand that occurred so many years ago with a man that lived in another state had moved to her town and had been working with her husband for about 6 months. I asked how did she find this out, she explained that it was a big company but at a company retreat there had been pictures taken and she had seen them and to her surprised that mistake of so many years ago was standing next to her husband.

He told her about some new coworkers and pointed to him, there was no doubt even the same name. She asked me what she should do, I told her there was no easy answer and she began to cry. I told her of some things she could do to clean the energy in hopes that if the confrontation occurred it might go easy. She wrote down the information and I will wait for her to call me and tell me how it resolved itself. I continued to give her a full reading and all was good so at the end I told her that I felt it would happen, the problem that is, but the solution would not be as bad as she thought. By doing all the things she had done all these years I felt she had mitigated that sentence forecasted so many years before by another person like me. The moral of the story is that although things come to pass there are always possibilities to change the outcome or even skirt certain destinies all together.

Hello Hector......

To the Point

I had a reading with you yesterday for the first time, and I just want to say that I was very impressed with your ability. At first I was bit skeptical about doing a phone reading, but it was jaw dropping amazing. I can't believe how you were calling out the names of people in my life etc...Amazing!! May God always bless you. Thank you for being one of the good people of light working for good on this planet. I would like very much to be added to your mailing list. I am also going to get your book. I will most certainly seek out one of your other services soon.

Smiles,

Sara Del Sol

Reunited

I am a true believer in spirituality, and I know that things happen exactly when they are supposed to. When I met Hector my friend had been begging me to go see him. She could tell that I was in a very deep depression and simply just felt lost. When I finally made the appointment, I couldn't sleep. I was so anxious of what he would say, or what he would do. When I arrived that morning I parked my car and seriously thought of just driving away! My anxiety was so high... I am so glad I built up the courage and got off my car and met with Hector! I cannot put into words how that day has helped my life. He is amazing, talented and yet down to earth. Genuinely good person.... The first thing he ask me was "who's James" my husband that has been dead for over 7 years. He talked to me about so many things, my father who is also deceased he asked about by name. Not only did he know about my spirits that surround me but he gave me great advice on how to control my anxiety. I am forever grateful! I brag about him to everyone, and I will meet with him again. Thank you Hector.

Many Blessings,

Chimerakis

Sent from my iPhone=

Texas connection

I got a call from a new client, unfortunately that day I was at the hospital doing a healing and had to re-schedule her for the afternoon. When we finally got talking I saw rail road tracks, or the double R's so she explained her first and middle names were R but she has the middle name nowhere. I further told her that she had at least 4 people around her with the R as the first letter In their first name. The mother, father, and two other significant relatives including a deceased relative. She wanted to go straight into romance so I asked her for a name I felt and she said correct that was her X boyfriend. I told her to stop looking for him as he was bi-polar, he was a drain, he was angry, and I don't believe I have heard one positive thing about him. She agreed with all of it and still asked me if he would be coming back. It is those clients that drain my patience; they want what they want and are willing to do anything to obtain it. After the spirit of a deceased relative came through the client was much more accepting of moving on, the message was rough and direct to stop wasting time with nonsense, even dangerous relationships. It's incredible the power the dead have over the living, all the info I gave and nothing one message from the other side and the client was on board with all I was saying.

The shift

> Hello!

Here it goes:

My entire experience with Hector is such a Blessed one, I am so grateful! I feel fortunate that I met him & so honored that he plays an active role in my life. It's like God gave me him as my human guardian angel. Hector has is very busy, but you would never know that. Because he is always fully present & engaged with you. Makes you feel important & like you are his only client. He literally has always been there for me. He knows when I'm feeling down or need a friend & he calls me to chat. He knows when I'm feeling so great & happy & he calls me to chat. He never reveals to me my lesson or the thing I need to discover. But acts as a light aiding me towards it. And he waits patiently for me to discover it. When I do (mind you I didn't even know I had lessons to learn in the 1st place) I call him so excited saying "Hector I figured out the problem or solution to whatever it was..." And then he finishes my sentence!! Because he knew all along!!! We have a lil joke when things like that happen; Ill tell him "What are you psychic?" And we laugh. He completely amazes me. I can be hard headed at times & some lessons have taking many years, but he always knows!

Hector has an amazing presents about him. You feel safe & welcomed. It's like you become aware of your inner peace. It's really beautiful. And that's just from being around him!

Hector has giving me the insights on people & situations that has helped me make my best choice about them. He never pushes or demands you do. He guides, sometimes warns, but always lets you do as you wish. Times I swear I know better (being young & thinking I knew everything) & I don't listen to him; after the fact he kindly tells me "well I told you so"!!

One of the greatest experiences I had was when I was driving home from work & I had an aha moment. What I felt maybe my biggest lesson yet: I suddenly became aware of what it was that Hector did for me that helped me connect with my path/ myself/ God. He loved & supported me according to my needs. According to Me, who I was/Am. Not according to any standards or labels. Literally for no reason or personal gain he gave to me as I needed. He didn't judge my lows, praised my highs, made me feel loved/ cared for, not afraid of him knowing my all ugliness, because I knew he accepted me. I feel safe with him & know I can trust him. He was gentle & firm with me when it needed it. He loved me through it all! Hector truly opened my eyes to loving one unconditionally & he gave me the experience of being unconditionally loved!

Hector has great & amazing powers! He has giving me many healings, clearings, & readings that have positively impacted my life!! He always gave unto me what I needed when I needed.

As a result from my relationship with Hector; I have a strong urge to seek the Truth, to want to know who I am, & live a life according to Me. What I want. No longer just getting by or surviving. I am in tune with my inner needs & work to be at peace. This is a priceless gift! I truly understand & know this. Everything in the physical world does not amount to what Hector has done for me!

B. Williams

Intruder in the house

I had an opportunity to visit an old house in Coral Gables Florida during the course of a cleansing. A client recommended me to them as a person that can fumigate as she put it all the dark energies infesting the home of an elderly couple. As soon as I arrived I could see this dark oozing energy all over the old house. It was in original condition but well kept, as I knocked at the front door I could see entities looking out the windows. Oh boy this was going to be one of those cleansings; they immediately opened the door and were very cordial in their greeting. They told me all that my client had told them about me and I was very flattered telling them I hope to be able enough to help them as I had her.

As I entered all I could see was the darkness that covered this otherwise beautiful estate home. It appeared they were believers as they had all kinds of relics with energy, ritualistic energies. I said nothing to them and continued to observe, they asked me where I would like to begin, so I asked for the kitchen. There are many different ways to deal with haunted houses so I would try first with camphor. I asked for a deep pot and placed many cubes of camphor and placed over burner to evaporate or liquefy. In either case the fumes it lets out is often enough to cut through the densest of spiritual fogs. After the fumes started to go up I grabbed the handle and started to walk the home. I asked the clients if they would take me around the home as if they were showing it to friends.

Once I finished the first floor I returned to the kitchen and heated my stuff again, remember this is a solid that changes into a liquid then evaporates. So once again I walked but this time the bottom of the home; as I walk I always pray for light and ask for all heavenly angels come to my aid, angels and archangels of the divine commission help me. Sooner or later I start to feel their assistance and this is one of those homes I truly could use it. Once I was half way done with the downstairs rock and roll the extra juice came in and I felt super charged. It's kind of a runners high when the second wind comes over you there is no stopping and you fill replenished. So it was that soon enough I was done with the camphor part of the cleanse. The gentleman asked so how is it going, I told him slow as there was a lot of strange stuff in this home. He said "you bet you" and smiled, I know that smile it is of someone that knows what they are talking about but is not ready to talk about it in detail.

Once I was done I told him I needed to go out to the car, I picked up some gun powder and my portable cigar holder. I asked the wife If I could have a glass of water and a place in the back yard I could use to clean them individually. She complied and told the husband "you first honey", he smiled that funny smile again and headed out with me. I explained how I clean and what I do so he would not be caught off guard. Arriving at the chair he was to sit for my cleaning the right side of the chair just collapsed by itself before the man could even sit down. I could tell he was surprised so I told him let's just get the other chair, he agreed and we began the cleaning, I started by cleaning his aura with a black cloth soaked in my own mix. I would cover the back and snap it off, then continued in a counterclockwise direction until I finished. Then I cleaned him with a mix of gunpowder, camphor and other powders, a cocktail that really packs a wallop. By the time I was done the person already felt lighter, I handed him a bath I had prepared in an empty milk gallon container and asked him to go to the shower and pour it over his head, allowing it to drape his body then he should just dry off. The person agreed and I headed inside to get the wife, she seemed to be talking but I did not see anyone else. I'm thinking she was speaking to the dead so I continued as if I did not notice. She was very nice as soon as I saw what was happening I sprayed her with this mix to break the connection and she asked why I had done this. I explained that until we figure out what was good and or bad I would just get rid of it all. She seemed to understand and I continued, while in the proses of cleaning her spirit of a woman came and gave her several messages.

The quiet ones

Along all of us there are some energies some good some not so good, so how do we know what is our own thought proses and when are we being guided or misguided by some of these other energies. Good question; happens more often than we would like, do we always know, not by a long shot. Here is an example of a situation that is the rule rather than the exception on this planet earth. A very nice couple, married for over twenty years, they were in crisis, someone recommended me so they asked me to come and cleanse their home. After speaking with them I decided this would be an interesting cleanse, over the last six months both were off in the way they felt towards each other. If you have been in a long relationship I'm sure you know the ups and downs in normal relationships but this was out of character. Their relationship was strong enough for them to realize there are other forces at work causing some of the fights they were having. Even their feelings were out of control, some of the emotions they were experiencing were very negative towards each other, even when there had been no problems they realized after dialoging about it that it was bordering on hate for no reason.

As suspected when I arrived there was a couple of spirits that had moved in, for some reason they targeted this nice couple for a breakup. In a case like this it's very important the couple realize it's not them and I gave them that confirmation right away as the two inter-loafers were not very nice and told me I should leave and never return. Cool beans I told the male spirit but not happening; he immediately made himself disappear, they can do that. Remember in the spirit world they have many powers and one of them is to show themselves and the other is to disappear at will. No time, no limit as far as these type of spirits go, they have the power to influence us and even manipulate our moods.

There is a balance in the world, the living or the dead all have to live in the big picture; you can always switch sides and either will accept you no matter the past. Much like our world, how many good people turn to crime, some in crisis others just because opportunities presented and they liked that life enough that stayed there. As I've told many clients that are lest say shady, that's right everyone deserves opportunities so I don't judge I just say what I'm being shown. I always harp upon those that the universe is balance so if they decide to stick their hands in the till to steal they should not make a habit of it for sooner or later they all get caught. I'm not suggesting doing it but if it happens and you are lucky enough to get away with it stop and reverse course to mainstream society.

There are angels and demons that walk amongst us, live I like to say we all have to wolves, who wins is simple the one we feed the most. So if we do good we become good if we do bad we become bd. Much like the food we eat, if good then we are healthy if not sooner or later your cholesterol goes up and start having health issues. Granted good living does not guarantee health but rather makes your chances better at a healthy productive life. Genes can affect no matter the lifestyle so if your ancestors have had kidney issues you might have to go above and beyond to lessen the chances those poor genes will bite you as you grow older.

Never abandon belief, if you believe your opportunities to live a better life is always greater. I don't mean pray without faith but rather believe in your heart and soul and the energy you will create will carry you through tough times instead of those who have no faith and collapse at the first years of adversity. Believe you are part of a greater universe and creator and you might surf those waves. I'd rather fly with the wind than against it; so it is with faith, if millions of people have faith and pray they are creating an energy movement. If you join it even on your own it works, you don't have to belong to a church or other group that believes in good to enjoy the rewards once it builds momentum like a big wave you can ride it and enjoy its strength.

Prayer is energy, does not matter the time of day or night any time is a good time and we can often feel that elation when truly in the prayer groove. Ask for help when you need it, you are not alone and often by asking friends and family to pray for you in difficult situations may mitigate those circumstances. I know when I'm challenged with a difficult task to help someone who is truly in darkness I will send out a 911 through email or other means and believe me I feel the boost of power. It's like a vitamin injection, over the years I've fine-tuned that asking part of my work and many otherwise difficult tasks have been successful without any major work from me. Nothing last forever but a push is a push when needed it makes the difference between an operation that only has a 20% chance of success for example or a dangerous trip. Even when having problems with another if you ask for guidance and prayer not only from the spirit realm but from the living your chances of success will be exponentially increased. Satisfaction is key to a loving life, always do your best, envision your dream, articulate it, passionately own it, be relentless, it's your movie. Try and never tie your dreams to a person or thing, a goal is much healthier; be stubborn in the pursuit of your chosen path. The more intensity you give your goals the better rooted they will be in your subconscious, this is the direct path to making it reality; but remember if you don't start today I guarantee you will not be finished any time soon so get on with implementation!

I cannot emphasize enough on becoming self-aware; this is where I recommend meditation and prayer on a regular basis. Those quiet voices that often inspire us to do wrong are always listening and when we are at our weak point they whisper in attempts to bring us over the edge. If we are comfortable with who we are then it becomes easier to realize when other forces are being influenced against us and who we are. At that time you need most of all to increase daily prayer and ask God for help, he will listen. We are all important and if we but ask we shall receive. Most of us travel our lives and never get first hand contact with these negative forces rather subtle and unnoticed we are diverted from our true path. If you are honest with yourself and think back there have been moments where you acted out of character and later you were angry at yourself for reacting the wrong way. Those and many other moments are situations where those dark forces attempt to sway us to do bad and taint us to become our worse instead of our best. By the same token many times we are given guidance and we see how unexpectantly we become our better selves.

Just the other day I was with my wife picking up some soup for our youngest who was sick, there was a lady selling flowers and my wife asked to buy some sunflowers. I did and handed her a three dollar tip for no reason other than it was a Sunday and she was out there working, attempting to make an honest living. I handed the flowers to my wife who stayed in the car and entered the restaurant to pick up the soup. On my way out she called me over and handed me some pompons and said bless you for your kindness. How about that, a simple act of kindness was rewarded by this lady. I told my wife what I had done and how she gave me those free flowers and sent a blessing my way. Hey good stuff, I'm still feeling good about myself for that situation. I would call that a miracle, they don't have to be life altering but it's a realization that there is still plenty good in this planet. The real voyage of discovery begins when we lose sight of the shore and view life with new eyes; remember perception is everything, sometimes it's good to remember to look at life as unique for each of us!

The tag along

My friend Larry called me to tell me a story of something that happened in his home a few nights before. He said it was 2am when the alarm sounded in the house, he got up an walked to the panel where it showed the front door had been opened. He checked but it was locked and no one seemed to be around the house, it was just he and his wife and they were both asleep so he reset the alarm and as he was turning it showed movement in the living room so he ran there and a door on the opposite side of the room seemed like it had just been closed as he walked in. He headed to that room with no other exit points but it was empty. I told him there was a ghost in the house and if very materialized the sensors can detect them. I focused and I saw the spirit, it gave me his name and told me my friend's wife looked like his wife so he had come back with her.

Larry told his wife and she was mortified at the idea that a spirit would just follow her home and stay living there. I described it as a heavy set man, after he told the family the son said that a few nights before he awoke thinking someone was in the room and he glimpsed a heavy set man living his room. He got up right away and no one was there so he had assumed he was just dreaming and did not make any more of it. They made an appointment and I headed for their home to clear out the intruder. I started with the home then Larry and no big deal but when I cleaned the wife what I found was more than expected. It had been with them for several years and as it happened to be she had not been able to find employment for several years. I told her about a moment when they were in the bedroom being intimate and after wards she thought the experience felt weird. She confirmed and wondered how I could have known this that had just happened recently. I explained that one of the spirits would sit in the room and observe them. She was freaked out and even more when I cleared it up that there was more than one attachment to her.

Well by the time I was done she was wiped out and slept for an hour, even some low back pain she had been having for days disappeared. That's right energy can cause very physical manifestations such as real pain. Its just energy so applied to an area definitely to results can be very destructive to the physical body. She joked and asked me if I could make her a size 2 again, I told her that magic she can create by not stuffing her face and working out. They laughed and thanked me for the weekend visit, I told her to keep an eye because even though I had done this those types of spirits so attached could come back. It's been a while and no more finding closed doors open or glasses out in the mornings so I'm confident the intruders hit the road for good.

Upset

I sometimes feel ready for more but this incident taught me perhaps they know best, I was at the park with my dog, it's a pit-bull my wife gave me as a present for father's day. I love the little girl, well she is now 54 pounds and she is six months old but very loving dog, not at all as pit bulls have being portrayed in the media. As you know most creatures adapt to their environment and it is those who push them to fight, to bring out the aggressive tendencies that are at fault and the animal. So back to it, I've had her trained for obedience and this was a class to make them social with other dogs; there was a woman in the class that was very anti my dog. She began to bad mouth my type of dog, pit bulls that is in spite of most of the group who are all dog lovers. There were attempts to explain that the animal is not at fault but the people who breed them to fight are the ones who create the monster. After about half an hour of her mouth I got upset and gave her a headache, she soon left and the rest of the group felt alleviated at her leaving. That does not make it right that I lost my tempter and gave her a skull crushing headache. I must learn to better leave things alone and not use my gifts for these cheap and unnecessary uses.

The new client

I just did a wonderful cleanse for a client sent to me by an attorney client of mine; she's a divorce attorney and has sent me at least 15 clients for help or guidance. This one in particular was a nice cleanse as from the beginning as she entered my home she came along with not one but three family spirits and a tag along. I mean a tag along because it was a spirit that wanted to give a message about her soon to be x husband. He, I mean the husband was not a very nice man and had done much harm to this nice lady. Anyway we started, I explained what I do from a to z because she had never gone to anyone like me; actually she said she had never even had her cards read but the attorney had recommended me so she gave it a try. She was honest so I wanted her to get the full service; I explained how I use a cigar and smoke it around the person, how it burns tells me a story that allows me to understand where she is and better guide me as to what I need to do. I on that day had some plants to clean her energy. I explained that plants pick up on everything that does not belong and absorbs it.

In her case I did not feel she needed strong stuff like gunpowder or sulfur or any of the many other modalities I use on occasion. I began by asking her who this older woman that was around her was, I gave her a name and approximate age the spirit had died. Right away she knew it was the mother. Along with her came her grandmother from the father's side and I believe an uncle. You must understand I see a lot of people and as soon as I'm done I begin to erase from my mind the event this is how I stay sane. Can you imagine if I would keep all that stuff in my head, no way so shaking it off is the best way all of us that practice can stay grounded and not go crazy.

I gave her some messages from each and reminded her about when she was young and her hair was down to her low back. She laughed, she now had hair very short, I told her about her liver and her drinking. She agreed and told me although she would drink to forget, she had stopped a month before. I suggested acupuncture to balance the liver weakness and allow her energy to recuperate. I gave her some guidance on the health front and she was in awe that I could see all that stuff without any blood work or any other medical inspection. I told her it's good to have a communicative spirit that guides me. I told her about one of the sisters and that she lived in another state and yet another sister by name and her issues. She really lost it when speaking about the young sister as I felt this heaviness on her face. So I expressed what I was feeling a pain in the face area and difficulties breathing. She explained a few days before someone had punched the sister in the face and she was in pain and her nose was still stuffed from the incident and earlier that day she had told my her how she was having difficulties breathing.

I continued and on one of the sisters was the spirit of the other grandmother, she explained she lived with her so no wonder her grandmothers energy was close to her. I asked about the grandmother that was with her and the state she showed me was where she was born. As I continued the cigar was showing me what a nice soul she had, she was just beat down by this obviously abusive person. Incredible how her spirits were pushing for her to move on and leave this nasty person in her rear view mirror. I gave her a bath to pour after she showers and some other instructions. At the end she was so impressed she paid for the sister with the punch to get a reading the next day. Oh yea the tag along, this spirit had a message for the nasty x husband, he would have some issues that could lead to a heart attack if he did not take better care. We agreed this was no longer her problem and I told the spirit to find other means to ask for help she was done with him.

The will

This was over a long period of time, a good client of mine was always concerned about money and if the x husband was prepared to take care of their children.

The most I could tell her was that his health was not well and heart or circulatory problems were all around him. She asked what did that mean, I explained that if he did not take care of himself he would or could die before his time. She kept in touch with him although he lived in a different country but she claimed he seemed in good health. For the stretch of a year or so it would always come out in the cards that this man, her former husband would have some serious health issues and if he did not take care could die early. I explained that he did not seem to have his things in order and this could become an issue for the assets later on. You must realize he was a wealthy man and had been married before my client and although he had two kids with her he also had grown children with the previous family and they lived in this other country where he resided. One day I got a call from her that her kids were visiting the father for a couple of weeks in the summer and they woke up to find him dead in the kitchen. I felt bad if for no other reason that the kids both minors were to witness such a chocking thing. As soon as it happened she called and started to check on what was left for the children. A bit callas but a necessary evil as he was not the most organized man.

She now was in a run for the kid's future, she had been made aware by some mutual friends that he had been drinking a lot and was out of control with regards to relationships. After much research and a trip to this other country she, my client realized that the other or previous family had control of most of his assets and her kids would be out of most of the money. It's been six months since the death and still nothing to prove he left them anything. During a reading he came through and told her there were several things he had left for the kids and he was very disappointed on how his other family was acting and shutting her and the kids out of his will. He said that there was some money in a life insurance only for her kids and she would get it. He told me to tell her to look for it as he from his site would do what he could to help and apologized again. It's only been another 30 days from this reading and the paper popped up and they would be getting an additional couple of hundred thousand dollars.

Wishful thinking

It was an old client of mine who called asking for permission to go on a trip to Vegas with a married man. I told her she was an adult and should do what her own mind was okay with and not look for redemption from me or the spirits. She was easy to do what was convenient with her and no matter what I said she would do as she thought so why should I give her council she was not going to listen to. I told her to just do what she thought she could leave with, after all this was not a life altering thing for her anyway. The guy I told her was just looking for a good time with a good looking girl; he was 20 years older than her and let's face it not in her league at all.

She agreed with all I said and asked me to look into the trip if she was going to enjoy it and if she was going to be safe. After all she did not really know this guy, so she gave me the guys information and told me she would email me when she left and when she would be back, so if she did not email me I should call the police. I told her not the be so dramatic as she would not have any issues with this man, he only wanted what most men in his position wanted, a good time. If she was okay with all of this then no problem and he would be careful not to step outside any lines she was not comfortable with. All this seemed to make her at ease so she agreed with him and they left for Vegas, the whole trip was only a three days adventure so it would be fine I confirmed for her. I told her to do some baths before to make sure her energies were at her best and she would have a good time. I got that return email so no calls to police and she did not even sleep with the man as I had said he just wanted the company of a beautiful woman and anything else he got was gravy.

Venom

It was a long time since I had read someone who was into snakes, so when I read this woman the snake significance was easy to spot. I told her that there seemed to be references to snakes around her. She was genuinely stunned that I would pick up on this hobby, she confirmed that she had a room full of snakes. She was into reptiles she explained, clarifying since she was a child snakes were her favorites. I spoke with her at length about her hobby and how she need to take care because I saw several poisonous species. She confirmed all this and asked if she would ever het one specific snake she had been wanting, I told her she would find what she was looking for in the form of a trade. I asked her if she had a water snake, specifically an ocean poisonous one. She was amazed and told me she has had that particular snake for over a year; I explained that the person that had the snake she wanted would trade for that one. Along with many other things I told her she was very satisfied with the reading.

Many months later I got a call from her for another reading, I told her if all she had was one question she should just ask and not to worry about scheduling the reading. She was very grateful because in truth it was just one question as I had stated. She wanted to know if she should trade the snake for the one she wanted and it was happening just as I had forecasted those many months ago. I suggested not waiting and do it as the guy might change her mind, she agreed and on the very next day the trade was done. She sent me a text two days after that the guy had changed his mind and wanted the snake back but she did not do it, in other words she kept the trade and the snake she had always wanted.

I got a call much like any other, wanting to schedule a reading. Most of my readings are over the phone and at least 80% of those are referrals from other clients. Over the years I've developed a good reputation so I do get the occasional web surfer who found me through sites that rank psychics or mediums. I never got to find out where this one came from since it was the first one in fourteen years doing this that I told the person I would not read her as she had done so much harm the spirits were not interested in helping her. The funny thing is that she did not reject the statement; she simply told me I understand and hung up the phone. Curiosity is a killer so upon my hanging up the phone I looked at the call log just to see where the call came from. You must remember I get calls from all over the world and I was a little curious as to who this person was. Unfortunately the caller I.D. said unknown so I stayed with the curiosity.

Upon reflexion I realized that there must have been something terribly wrong with this person because I've read all kinds, good and bad and I've always been lead to believe that no matter we must give all a chance for redemption. The job is not to fix the person but to sprinkle some hope that there is no matter the situation a chance to make better or change for the better, that there is always hope. So for my spirits to one by one show me how they turned their backs to the person there had to have been more to it than simply she was bad. Once I had some time to absorb what had happened I asked one of the spirits I work with why. I was so surprised at the answer he gave me, she was a dark entity, I inquired further what he meant by this he explained that there are people like me but their whole existence was to work for the darkness. She was one of those and part of her job was to corrupt or to suck dry people like me. Not all would have seen her true nature and once engaged she would have attached herself and infiltrated my life in such a way as to damage me any way she could. He further explained that they are not frontal attack types but rather snakes that attach and slowly take the life force or corrupt it until they are out of the game, one way or another.

The rough path

There are many paths, as many as there are people, most choose the path they want some are karmically motivated in certain directions. So I want to bring to light one such case and it will be for you to choose if karma or choice that has embarked the course for this person. She came to me one day for a reading, throughout the entire reading I was getting very conflicting views of this person. I don't mind telling you I was a bit frustrated as the views were so different it was as if I was looking at two people. If you remember I look at people's futures in terms of windows the strongest ones have the better possibility of manifesting into the future for them, the better future that is. In the case of this woman I was visualizing her as a type of person and her future and past were showing me a very different type of person. Here is the thing about the future, when you look at it, change is what can occur, so I'm very careful what to say or not say; most of what I'm shown is personal information so I can better understand the person I'm helping.

She read to me as a typical or textbook future for a typical woman, love romance, hard worker, all the typical female energies were there. However for me her future and past showed tragedy, death, murder, violence, well you get the idea and my conflict. I get information quickly so all this I had told you was in the first few minutes of the reading. I wanted to get a grip on her so I gave her a description of her physical to ground myself in something concrete before I continued. I figured If she did look like I saw then maybe everything else was accurate and I just had to decipher the weird past and future stuff. Well she felt I was looking at a Facebook picture or something as I described her. So after receiving this complication I told her about some medical stuff and asked her if I also looked at her medical history chart from the doctor's office. I can appreciate a little doubt as most mediums don't get information as I do but I also feel you should give me the benefit of the doubt and as I give information that there is no way I could have looked up then make up your own choice as to the veracity of the information. I continued by telling her about a project she had in her mind but had not discussed with anyone as of yet. In other words I gave her enough to reassure her I was in deed looking beyond and not on some sort of web site as she had originally insinuated.

Once we were on the right page I was able to continue what was already a strange read from a psychic's point of view. By now we were at least on the same page of discovery and I began to throw at her some of what I perceived as stranger information. You must understand I do many readings and there are some clients who tell me they only want to hear the good stuff; others tell me don't color it just give it to me as it comes so this one lady just needed help and did not care what came out as long as she got some answers, it will be up to you at the end of this story to decide what to believe. By this I mean how to look at the information as from the beginning I told you my views or perception as to where all this is coming from.

Besides the obvious of her look and feel and medical information I began to tell her about the darkness that pursued her. I told her of a spirit that passed from a violent encounter, I told her I felt impacts to the chest and back and a drop to the floor in what seemed to be a dark place, perhaps at night but in like an alley way. She confirmed the man, oh yea I also gave her the person's name, she explained he had died from gunshots to the back and it was in an underground garage and he was found face down in a pool of blood. I told her about the fast car she confirmed he had such a car and I also told her he was doing illegal activities and was killed or betrayed by someone he knew. She confirmed the person who had him killed was someone who had worked for him. As this is a case that has not yet found resolution I will abstain from certain facts I told her so as to not taint any ongoing investigation.

He gave her a message and thanked me for helping her; she understood the message and asked me why he had not gone into the light. From what I perceived from this spirit he was kind of vulgar, rough and tough so my interpretation was that until he found justice he would remain and help those looking for the truth to catch the person who had orchestrate his demise. He seemed frustrated as he always covered his tracks and was blindsided by someone he trusted and did not expect. She told me he was very to himself and did not trust many so she could understand his reasons for not moving on.

He spoke to her in his own words, words she found familiar and emotional at the same time to move on from this and not to delve in something dangerous as he loved her and wanted her safe. Immediately the scene changed and another man this one on horseback arrived at a distance. She immediately recognized who it was and again she was surprised, no longer having doubts as to my information. Oh yea one detail all of this happened in another country not the United States so even more unbelievable to her that I could see it. Back to the second spirit, she explained he was a cowboy. I told her that he suffered a similar death in other words violent; she confirmed he passed also from gunshot wounds.

I paused and she asked if I was still on the phone, remember my readings are telephonically only doing personally clearings or cleansings of energy. I snapped back because the spirit was showing me something so I explained what I was shown. I told her how the spirit had also been less than clean, by this I mean he was doing illegal things. He had shown me how he stole money from someone and they had him killed for it. I told her that this was different than the first person as this person was about drugs and the other was not. She confirmed this to be true as well, the cowboy told her a few things that lead me to believe he was not the brightest person and she confirmed that he was not like the other one.

I've cleaned her since that initial reading as we agreed that most of those energies no longer belonged and although they were not harming her they were very low level spirits stuck here in this planet and can only hold her back or disrupt her energy. Once she came I realized she again was involved in a relationship with someone whom did illicit business. She confirmed smiling so I asked her why, she told me they just gravitate to her. I told her no, firmly and without a second thought she was attracting that type because she like the fly liked close to the fire and sooner or later like the fly she would get burned. I asked her to stand in the middle of cleaning her energy and asked her to turn around like a 360 degrees. She did and I told her have you considered that maybe she liked the dangerous types because she was dressed very provocative or at the very least her clothing said I'm hot and I know it.

I told her beauty is a season that if we are lucky and blessed with it should enjoy and make the most of it for our experiences, but not abuse the gift by living dangerously just because we can. I asked about her youth, especially the relationship between mother and father, she explained that the mom was the boss and manipulated the father. I asked how her relationship was with the father, she said great. I told her let me guess the one with your mother has always been strained to say the least she confirmed this. I told her, her mother was probably the type who always wanted and got what she wanted no matter the expense and or whomever she had to use. Again she confirmed she was not a very loving mother but did use everybody to maintain a certain lifestyle and status.

We finished this cleanse but I told her there was so much to do that it would probably be an ongoing thing with the cleansings until all or most of the baggage was gone. I explained that it did not matter how bad the energy if you catch it quickly enough it's relatively easy to release but if like her it's been a lifetime then likewise with any decease it will take longer to reverse the effects. She is a smart woman and understood what I was saying so we agreed to meet in a couple of weeks again for a follow-up cleanse and to see how things were going with her. I reminded her as I walked her to her car that she needed to cut ties with this new lover as part of changing gears is also changing habits. She laughed and promised to do just that because she truly wanted to change her life for the better.

A couple of weeks later she came back with some closure from the past, but still her energy promoted complications in the relationship department. She has a business and this was doing good so in that aspect of her life I felt no need to do anything but keep her clean so all would see her as a hard working professional who accomplishes her task. I asked her who the married man was, she said someone interested in her. I reminded her about keeping to people who are not problematic, she refreshed my memory telling me that what in fact I had warned her about were dangerous people and this guy was not dangerous. I told her that he is dangerous, perhaps not deadly dangerous, and I said perhaps because you never know how things work out in a triangle.

I'm still cleaning her to this date but don't feel she has yet mastered the idea of looking for the right person. I can only hope with time and luck she can overcome these short comings, as she is really a nice lady who has this flaw. As of today she is now dating another dangerous man who again as the others does not even leave close to her but keeps her in comfort and wealth. Some have it but don't know how to apply it, she has that intangible quality that makes her appealing but she like many does not know how to take it for a spin in the right venue. I can only hope she can stay alive long enough to get out of this and find the right and uncomplicated man in her life!

A mentor's tale

People think that those who do what I do live a charmed life, quite the contrary as I will show you in this story. A very good friend of mine and mentor, she was the very first person that I saw to get a reading. It was funny I told the story in my first book about her so I will not go into details in this one. Suffice to know after all these years she is still my friend and we have made a ritual to read each other once a year as we just did this January. It was a very good year and she told me about the past year and this coming one. I'm very excited as it all sounded good; on the other hand her cards were less than pristine. She had a couple of attachments that were causing havoc in her daily life. I described what I was feeling and she said that it was exactly what was going on in her life.

She had always wanted to be in politics in the municipality where she lives but was being blocked by a powerful political who got his start there. He kind of looked out for his roots and felt she was not the kind of person he would like to be a counsel woman there. He made sure the Mayor and other positions knew that if they allowed it he would pull his support; so they did what they had to and blocked her every election. In my opinion they even pulled votes so she would not have enough. Anyway, after I read her I told her to come get cleaned as you know by now cleaning is like bathing, if you don't take a shower well you know; so it is with energy and with people like us even more because we can always get something from the people we are cleaning. Yes, she needed it badly, you know how it is; we do for others and sometimes forget or get lazy for ourselves. How many know a handy man or plumber or carpenter and he has things pending in his own home. The same when we get home sometimes we are just tired and don't want to do what needs to be done.

The thing about energy, especially the negative kind is that with time it gets worse, stronger that is. Like any stench if not cleaned after a while no one wants to stand close to you. No different with this, no matter how strong the spell or the negative energy it takes time to gain strength as it acclimates to your own frequency. So it does not matter if it's weak with time it will become strong and eventually overcome us if not dealt with promptly. So it was with her, some of this stuff on her had already been there for a while so I invited her to my house. As she is older I usually go to her for our readings not to inconvenience her. She agreed and the very next day she was there to get her cleaning. I told her many changes were coming and pulled her ears about keeping up with her energy work. She was getting lazy in her old age I told her and she had to keep the cleanings regular. She agreed and just told me as an excuse that it was just that she was getting old and she was tired of all the work. She sometimes sees 8 to 10 people a day and at her age it becomes sometimes exhausting. I know she also has diabetes and all these things can zap your strength but at this time I needed to give her tough love!

It's great when you clean someone like yourself because they can sense the energies and what is going on. While at my place I had to go into the house to do something and when I returned she told me my spirits thanked her for helping me and guiding me at the beginning. I thought that was cool. So I continued to clean the two spirits that were causing problems. I was not overly concerned with the one that was in her house as it stayed and did not come with her, it was more about the one causing the energy drain. Her emotions were on a roller-coaster and it needed to go, so as engaged her and made sure she took a hike. Spirits that are attached usually find some kind of affinity with the person attached to, so if you sower the mix they just move on.

She felt energized ad told me a day later how she was able to do all these things she was procrastinating before. This can go either way, she could have just as well felt very drained and recouped by the next day. One thing she told me was how she was going to buy some stuff I had told her she need to do a spell and she ran into one of the counsel men in her municipality. She was so excited because he approached her and told her to get ready as he was going to sponsor her to get on board with the city in the exact position she had always wanted. How about that, just what I told her; she was so excited and I was glad to have been a part of moving that energy for her to attain what she wanted. She now had a choice to make because one of the other things going on in her life was a possibility for a television series being filmed in Columbia where she would portray the mother of Celia Cruz, a very famous Latin singer. That was another story as she would have to relocate to Colombia for at least six months. The job was hers if she wanted it; sometimes you have to be careful what you wish for because when your ship comes in often it docks all at once and with all your wishes at once, there are choices to be made. Proof them wrong, stop being a spectator, participate, with enough time and nerve you can accomplish anything; no such thing as the perfect moment, life is too short for regrets just do it, don't wonder what if!

Series of events:

Thank you for everything :)

>

> Amy's experiences with Hector:

>

> The day I 1st met hector was in 2002; at the gym. The trainer I was working out with was like "oh there's that guy who's psychic, let's go talk to him & see if he really is". I was curious but didn't believe in it. We went up to him (probably rudely now that I think about it) asked if he could prove to us he's psychic. He asked for our names & birthdays. I don't remember what he told her, but he was able to tell me about my current relationship, exactly how I treated the guy, how certain things make me feel, weird shooting pains I would get on my back & the exact places I would get them. An abundant amount of perfect detail was pouring out of him. I was completely shocked & left speechless. Then he paused & asked me "who's Darren?" I was slow to answer & said the only Darren I know is dead. He said "who is he?". I said he's my cousin. Hector said that Darren wants to make sure that we know it was an accident, he didn't mean to shot himself. He was just messing around. He knows the death certificate says "suicide", but it was not. You see when I was 8 years old my cousin Darren put a gun inside his mouth & pulled the trigger. Died at a very young age, 19 or 20. His friend that was present at the time said he was playing

with the gun all night & that he was joking when he shot himself. I did not even know the death certificate said suicide. I later found out when I told my cousin his sister his message. Hector asked if we had any questions for him & I asked what is the name of the man of my dreams, the guy I will fall in love with. He said one of his names will start with M. Meeting Hector was an incredible experience!

>

> In 2012, 10 years later. I fell in love & his last name started with M. The funny thing is, when I realized I was in love with him I didn't even know his last name!!

>

> In 2013 I was driving in my car to an appointment for work. I was feeling very low & sad. I had just lost 3 accounts & 2 more wanted to cancel. And Hector calls me. I said Hi trying to act like all is well, but he knew & said to me "Amy what's the matter?" & tears started pouring down my face I tried to talk the best I could. I explained what was going on with work & how I felt like I was getting beating up. I told him I needed a cleanse. He agreed to meet with me that night after work.

> I wiped my tears & proceeded to my app. Well I sold them & with a very high priced product! I called Hector as soon as I left, cheering about my sale/ victory! He told me that he said a little prayer asking to give me a little break. I was so grateful he did that!

>

> Later after work I met with Hector. He cleaned me & gave me a bath to do when I got home. The next morning I had 4 appointments to give big presentations to all while my direct manager, my GM, & the VP sit in & watch me! I work as an advertising consultant. I sell adverting to car dealerships. So I sell to sharks! It's a challenging enough task as it is selling to them alone. I arrived 30 min early to the 1st app. I honestly was ready to vomit. My armpits were sweating & my heart was pounding. I was soooo nervous. All this while, sitting in my car in the parking lot of the dealership. My direct manager got there before the others & I just told him straight out. I think I'm gonna vomit! I showed him my wet armpits even!! He looked at me & said "relax, you're gonna do fine". Which didn't help me at all. I was ready to chuck up my breakfast all over my presentation. Finally the moment had come my GM & VP arrived & parked at the same time the dealer was ready to see us. Once in the conference room I started speaking & my voice was so shaky. I sounded insecure & weak. I stuttered (I never stutter) I was showing the wrong page that I was explaining. I mean it was awful. The worst presentation of my life. I'm really not ever that bad, I was just sooo nervous! But here's the thing: I sold the dealer. Signed the agreement right there. And when we left, in the parking lot the VP stopped a moment to give mc praise on how well I did. How professional I was & that he was so impressed with my presentation. My GM said I Nailed it & I did a great job.

My direct manager said really good job. As they were going on with their praise my performance; it was like time stopped & I was thinking "what the Fudge are these people talking about?!?" I could not believe it was real. I mean I really sucked & they were going on as if they were wearing rose colored glasses.

> At the 2nd app; I no longer wanted to vomit but still was nervous. This was a big shot dealership with the GM's big ego to match it. I gave the presentation not as bad as the 1st time, but I struggle to find any confidence & keep forgetting information. So I was drawing a blank throughout the whole presentation. Awful! Well guess what. The dealer signed!! And the dealer turned & started telling everyone what a great job I did & how impressed he was with me! Again outside they stood around me telling me how well I was doing & how well I interact with the dealers! All I was thinking is what's going on? That's when I realized: Hectors cleanse!!! This cleanse was so powerful! The intention of the cleansing was for me to bring in more money/ accounts & to really impress my upper management. Anytime I do a cleanse with Hector for more money/ accounts always within that same week new accounts come flooding in (management is never with me). But I thought I was going to impress everybody by actually doing well & showing my best. I am good at my job!! But it didn't matter how I did, they somehow in a very weird way (because it was very weird, at the time I didn't believe it) couldn't see my errors.

> The 3rd & the 4th apps. Both signed for the following month & both went on about what a great job I did! I was still trying to give a good presentation, but by this time I was aware of their faces & how they looked at me as if I did no wrong. And believe me I threw out wrong things because I just could not believe what was happening!!!!

> Immediately on my way home I called Hector to tell him about this craziness & the thank him because everything I asked for he delivered!!

>

> That night I felt an odd presents in my room. And all of a sudden I could hear someone saying something. I thought to myself am I going crazy? So I got up & went closer to the noise, in hopes to prove I'm not crazy! But I really heard someone talking & I said "what's going on?" Well what a mistake that was!!! Because then I had like 3 different voices trying to talk to me & they wouldn't shut up or go away. I started to cry & thought I've Fudging lost it. I began to pray & I prayed for Hector & his protective spirits to help me. All of a sudden like from a seen in the movies a gust of wind blew in my room. (All windows were shut) and I heard Hectors voice say "did you miss me" & then I heard him say in a firm tone "get out of her room" and then it went silent. One of the craziest days of my life!!

>

> The next morning my family & I went out for breakfast & I was sharing the events that took place the day before. Most were in awe. A few were trying to make a joke of it & said a comment "what does Hector do? Tell you it's ok I'm just going to pee on you & give you a golden shower." I rolled my eyes & didn't even want to energy to their nonsense!

> Later that evening Hector called me to chat. To my surprise before we hung up, he said to me "Amy just so you know, I never had to pee on anyone" I couldn't believe it!!! I was so embarrassed; I didn't even tell him what had happened! I just said oh cool, talk to you later bye!

>

> To this day I don't believe I have shared that with you: / But it's awesome how you knew!!!

Beth Williams

Miami

Sent from my iPad

The protector

This was a good day, I cleaned my wife as I do often but for the first time I channeled one of her spirits; not just one but Enrique, the one that always talks to me. We all have spirits but the only one of hers that communicates with me just like one of mine was cool. He took over; It was not anything I expected. I felt an entity around her so I let it in, this is how I channel the spirits and the best way to allow the ones that are stuck to realize they are free souls and they have no further need to be here on earth. If it had been a lost soul as I call them then my wife who knows how the proses works would have communicated with it and told it that it was borrowing a body and they should go to the light. It's like therapy for lost souls and usually they realize and move on. For example she would have told it to look and feel the body and awakened it from the displacement they were suffering by realizing it's not their body and usually this is enough to get the spirit to go into the light of God.

It was incredible she explained how the spirit came and opened my eyes and looked at everything. She asked who he was and he told her Enrique and hugged her, she loved how loving his energies were and how he was soft spoken and gave her some very impactful but personal messages. I know that some spirits are like that, open the mediums eyes but none of mine do it, so I was surprised. When I returned to consciousness my wife was very excited and happy and told me all the thing they spoke of and he also told her that he did not like the cigar as he believes its bad to smoke. He asked her of the word she uses to describe him and she told him, male chauvinist; he laughed and explained to her how he felt about all the ways that women in general were conducting themselves in this time and he was not totally sure if it was a good thing. He also told her of all the wonders that exist now. He looked around and found all of modern time to be wondrous time we live in. He laughed and told her that I was a bit chunky compared to the body he had, very skinny compared to me.

This was a very exciting moment for my wife to meet face to face with one of the spirits that have been with her since she was a little girl. He gave her messages about her life so she would understand and my wife was in awe. He told her he would not take too much time and he had never channeled through before because he knew his place and my spirits were always around. She was very curious that he opened my eyes and would look and touch all things around and I told her that some spirits are like that but none of mine do this so it was definitely different. She told me when he hugged her she felt the love in the hug and it made her feel warm all over, suffice it to say that as of this date it was the most emotional experience for her with relation to spirituality. I'm glad I was able to provide this experience for both of them, I told him after he left that my body would be available to him if he should choose to come through again to speak with her. He thanked me and then made himself invisible to me again; remember spirits can choose to manifest and also to remain anonymous to us humans.

The referral

Most of my business is referral, although lately I've been getting calls from people from all over the world that tell me they found me at web sites where people like me are rated and I had five stars. Cool stuff, but I still get 90% of my business just by word of mouth. In this situation it was curious as it was a person who had been through a lot over the last four months or so. I was referred by another person who does the same type of business as I do, once I spoke with the father who told me she had been through doctors, psychologist and been cleansed by at least four other people before getting to me. The diagnosis was mixed and nothing made sense to the family. She's in her twenties so she still lives at home and the family was very concerned at the fact that no one had figured out what was wrong with her. One doctor a psychiatrist felt she had a break down and he even suggested to file her as a disability case. Another said she had been sent some evil spirits, yet another person said she had attachments that want to make her crazy.

None of the people had helped her and the pills for the supposed depression were just making her like a zombie all day, those were the mother's words. I first spoke with the father over the phone and asked him if there was someone in his family who had a break down, he said his first cousin had been institutionalized. I asked about the mother and once I tuned in my first question was about her was who was the relative who died of the heart attack. He said her mother had passed from a heart attack, he asked why and I answered because when I tuned in that was the first spirit I felt around her. I decided to take the case and back to the home visit.

After the meet and great I turned to her older sister who was there by chance to visit the parents and told her she should not gain weight and she asked why. I explained the first spirit I felt was of a heavy set or fat man. The mother jumped and said that could be your grandfather who loved to eat. She continued to say the daughter loved food and had recently began eating too much. I told her for health reasons she should be careful and she said ok. I asked her for her birthday and told her she had recently been on a boat, she laughed and told me they had gone on a cruise recently. I told her the best place for her to let emotions out would be near the ocean. She confirmed how much she loved the ocean waters. I asked her a few more questions and discussed with her the way she was too jealous. The mother said yes she was a pistol and it did not take much for her to jump to conclusions. We all had a laugh and I turned my attention to the lady in question and the younger sister. I asked her for her birthday and asked her permission to look into her eyes, she thought it was a little weird but no worries. She began to be freaked out a bit when I told her about how she was full of shit, they laughed and said she was always constipated. I told her she felt toxic, especially in the intestinal area. I told her my diagnosis was that she had probably eaten something bad and never realizing it and the fact that she got constipated probably accelerated the infection.

I believe that this same infection or virus was the cause of her mental instability. I told them about the woman who came to me for a cleansing because she was worried about her son who was in a special class for kids that had attention deficit. I was able to help her by telling her to put him on a heavy dose of probiotics. I told her that whatever the dose on the bottle to double it for six months; further I told her every bottle he goes through the next one should be a different manufacturer. I explained not all have the same bacteria and it will be a better chance to find the right one and help him. She called me about four months later just to thank me and tell me how the teacher asked for a conference to tell her she did not know what the treatment was but the son she felt no longer needed to be in that type of class any longer.

I gave the girl a bath I had prepared with herbs and asked her to take a shower and do the salt and sugar scrub, then pour the bath over her head and dry off. Then I sat her down and cleaned her with a cigar, as I went along I would talk to her and to the parents to keep them busy and told them they could ask question if they had any. Half way through the cleaning I asked the girl to look at the cigar as I explained to her that I read how it burns. I pointed out to numerous wholes along the length of the cigar and two of them had within them what looked like eyes. She acknowledged what she saw and asked me what it all meant. I explained that each was the energy of a different soul around her and that unlike what she was told by others no one had intentionally or unintentionally sent her any dark souls. Instead I told her she was an undeveloped medium and all she was experiencing, the voices and all was just because that part of her was awakening.

Before I started to help me clear up the ambiance I placed up high a glass cup with water and a lit candle floating in it. I asked the commission of spirits that pick up turbulence to help me pick up any negative vibes allowing me to do what was needed and help this young woman. Well into the cleaning, when the relatives were there listening and asking questions the glass shattered, not fell, as the bottom was still there. It simply shattered from so much energy the cup was absorbing. Everyone was freaking out, I explained that this was one of the ways a person can clear an area of negative energy. You must understand it rarely explodes but at times where there is so much of it, it could happen and it did on this day.

I explained how spirits roam the earth and they are simply lost or displaced souls who did not move on to the astral world and cleared the web we are given when we have a body. She asked what that means, I told her that we choose the mission before and it usually means we cross paths with the same souls over and over. Unfortunately we have to move on to remember and those who stay behind after a while even forget they are no longer alive. So they find certain people like me as beacons because if you think about it they are walking around the living that do not see and for the most part can't even sense them. So when they find one that can it's like the moth to the fire, unfortunately it's not supposed to be like that so it can cause kind of a short circuit and can manifest to the living in many ways such as what she was going through and to a lesser degree just when you go into a room or a drawer to look for something you suddenly lose your train of thought and ask yourself why I'm I here, what was I looking for.

I finished the first cigar and I told her I would clean her with another just to see if it was all gone. The second was almost perfect burning as a cigar should, so then I asked her to stand and cleaned her with plants and a big handkerchief I use to finally clear out the aura from any residual energy. She told me when done that she was so sleepy and had no energy, she said she felt so relaxed she did not understand. I explained how when one does a cleansing and enough energy is taken from the body its normal to feel drained but soon she would regain her strength and the new energy would be fresh and clear of turbulence.

I asked the mother to take down some remedies that I wanted the daughter to do, she was ready and so I detailed the probiotics, vitamin B-12 in injection 1 cc once a week for six months or if she was scared of needles she could take sublingual B-12 anywhere from 3 to 6 per day. I also asked her to take an ice bath once a week for one month; she asked how that worked, I explained she needed a bath tub and she should fill with cold water only. Once she entered butt first her back should be against the wall and her legs hanging out the side. The only parts that can get wet was the midsection and nothing else, she needed to stay in there for 15 minutes and when she got out the midsection should be red or purple from how cold this should be. She should immediately wipe down with a towel from the legs up so the dripping water should not touch the dry parts.

I explained that was a proses because she had some chronic stuff in the intestinal area that needs healing. She would feel like a million dollars starting from the very first one she took. I suggested she start weaning off from the pills she was taking for the depression but she should speak with the doctor and ask him to set a regiment on how to do this. I explained that doing it cold turkey could have dire ramifications and only a doctor should guide her how to do this. The mother read off the list of thing and I confirmed that with all this she would no longer feel the way she had been feeling. I told her that when someone has a flu or worse even once it's over it might take the body a while to fully recover this was no different. They thanked me and said we hope this will be the last thing we would have to do to fix the situation. I told her to have faith and soon enough the daughter would be her same old self again.

Last Minute

I got a call late afternoon from a new client who wanted an appointment, so I told her a couple of days later in the afternoon. As I was going to finish the call a spirit from her side told me please it's urgent. I then told her if she would come this evening I could give her 8pm.

She agreed and I told her my cost and directions to my place, she said okay and I continued with my day. It was later that evening that she was coming she got lost and the reality is that finding my place is easy these are ways spirits influence the living so they cannot get the help they need. She called and I helped her, she was apologetic and soon after she arrived.

As we were walking to my backyard where I do some of my work I turned and asked her who this man talking to me was and I gave her his name. It was my father she said, I told her how he died and curiously enough some other unique stuff only she would acknowledge to be him. He was the spirit that told me that it was urgent, so I told her about her situation and the fact that she was at a cross roads in her life and her marriage. She told me that in spite of her been a professional and hardworking she was not getting ahead. I explained that what had been her past was not going to be her future, further I told her that was coming would balance out what she had gone thought in her life. She smiled and said since she had never been to someone like me she did go many years ago to someone who had done her natal chart for astrology and he had phrased it very similarly. Of course this was at a much younger age and at that time she would not have forecasted the hard life she would have. But now in her late forties she can see the validity of what that man had said and told me from my mouth to God's ears let it by as I say.

I continued telling her things about her family and kids including how one had asthma, the other was a medium who probably cried as a baby and said he could see things in the room. She was freaking out how I knew all these things, she was a Christian and they were not to believe in such things but I guess when the noose is around the neck most people would get help from where it comes from. She loved the session and then began to ask questions as I continued the cleansing. I like to talk while I do my things it tends to distract people allowing me to get in and do my thing. I found that otherwise they can create a block and the object is to help by shifting the energies back to where they should be.

We came to the conclusion that her husband's anger needs fixing and she had been dealing with many things from many people. I brought up her mother and the poor circulation and the varicose veins. I told her she was a very negative woman who lived in the past and would die if she did not start to live. She explained her father died young and the mother never remarried so she was in a sense alone. Recapping, the father had told me why did she ever marry this guy, well I did not tell her that since we know parents always know best and this woman looked beat up and not in need of a lecture. She asked if I could connect with her dead sister but unfortunately she was nowhere to be found. I explained to her that I cannot summon spirits but if they are around I can usually make that connection. Remember the dead want to talk and don't have the opportunity usually so any occasion they usually take it, to voice their messages.

The quickie

This reading was so quick that I will just touch on it; it's good to know that some days you are just on the money. It happens to all of us, including me; this person was a new client like most referred to me by another client. She called and from the beginning right after I answered the phone, oh yea just to remind you most of my readings are over the phone, I told her she was calling me for one reason and it was about two married men and I followed it with an x boyfriend that keeps coming back.

She told me I would think my friend told you something about me but she only knows about the one guy. I told her one of the men was local and the other out of state or at the very least very distant. She said that is right, by then I had her attention, so I continued by telling her I don't like this but since it appears you do don't fall for either men as I do not foresee leaving the wives. I do see the x-boyfriend continuing to knock on your door until you tell him no more. She laughed and said that's how it is but he keeps me entertained during dry seasons. I asked her if there was anything else about romance she said no, anything else I asked she said no this was it. Always remember when you are doing readings or being read wait for it, then when it seems the flow of information has ended is when you come out with your list. In my case by the time I'm done talking a good 75% of what the client called for should have come out without them opening their mouth. All the above info was disseminated in an 8 minute reading, I think the shortest reading I've ever had.

Unexpected visitors

This was not too bad, I started the reading with a question, who was this person; I described the person, how they died and the first name. My client immediately recognized it was her ex-husband's father. She told me how he was a nice man whom she got along with but she had not heard from the family if not to argue. There were overall three spirits and two were from her former husband's side of the family. I told her if she had been the bad one this would not be so and in my opinion it was his fault, the divorce that is. I spoke with her about the legal matter and she said there was a court hearing concerning a property settlement. I described some co-workers who were thinking about her by name; right away she knew who they were, we discussed some ailments about a family member who was not taking care of their health and about another trip to Europe.

She found it interesting how the current husband of many years had not come up, I reassured her it was about the spirits that were there but we would get to him. I told him how I felt him and about his drinking, she confirmed he had times throughout the year when he would lose focus and start drinking accessibly. I told her about the spirit that was poised with bags in hand to travel to Europe. She confirmed how she had been there many times and wanted to go again. She wanted to know about her health, I explained the spirits took me to who they felt might have upcoming health issues, the fact they did not take me there for her just reassures me that she was good to go as far as health. She agreed and expressed how she just wanted to know for sure. Along the way I named some states that she had significant with, some with the husband and some with her, all made sense and each fit the person I discussed with her. She was very excited about the reading and she said it did not disappoint and wondered when she should call again.

The Business

From the months of May through the end of August of 2013, my partner's business had slowed down tremendously. There was a far less flow of income coming to the business than previous months and previous years. He has owned his company for over 15 years and has a strong clientele that he offers multiple services to. It was unexplainable on why business had decreased by so much since his clients are major international companies with a strong global presence. By the end of July, the companies expenses started to pile up. For the first time in 15 years, he was almost certain the business would have no choice but to close its doors. The accumulated monthly debt was in the tens of thousands of dollars and the multiple real estate property debt was in the millions. The stress of losing it all was starting to take its toll on our family.

Since we cleanse our home frequently with sage, prayer, and holly water, I recommended to my partner that maybe we should do the same at the business. He was a little apprehensive at first, but then agreed for us to cleanse the energy at the business location. The next day, we went to his building and cleansed with sage, and prayed for a turnaround. After we cleansed the business location, we closed the business and disposed of what was left of the bundle of sage we had burned. With much faith in God, we were convinced things would get better.

Within days of the cleansing at the business location, things actually got worse for us. The monthly income generated from the business was still decreasing and our debt was dramatically increasing. At home, the energy was off between the both of us and arguments over petty things became more frequent and constant. Strange things started to happen in our home. The TV would turn on by itself when I was home alone and the volume at full blast. Our dog was acting uneasy, growling at certain areas of the house, and scared to enter our bedroom. By the end of the week, we became very angry with each other for no apparent reason and it felt like we were on the verge of separating. One night, after a very intense argument, I became extremely emotional. When we finally went to bed, I was having intense nightmares, talking and fighting in my sleep, and crying uncontrollably. My partner was freaked out and started to pray for us. As he would pray, he told me that my face looked like it had transformed and was possessed by something.

At that point, my partner called my mother to come to our house as he felt helpless and didn't know what to do. My mom came over immediately with a cigar, holly water, rosary beads, her bible, and agua Florida. Since she had known Hector from many years before, she had remembered cleansing advice Hector had given her in the past. After she cleansed our home, I felt much better but I knew something was still wrong. As we were talking in the living room after the cleansing, I noticed hand prints on our wall. These hand prints weren't there prior because we would have noticed them from since they were so visible. These prints were in strange places on the wall, some very high up close to the ceiling, others in corners that had home furnishings in front of. We were all speechless. My mother told me, "You have to call Hector" and then gave me his number. We immediately contacted Hector to make an appointment for a reading.

During the reading, Hector picked up on the financial troubles, us arguing over nothing, and had mentioned people's names that we knew. He also picked up my attempt of cleaning the business and told us that we had to spiritually cleanse ourselves since we hadn't done so correctly after the cleansing at the business. The negative energy had followed us back home and was creating havoc in our personal relationship. We were both so amazed since there was no way he had known about our personal rollercoaster ride we had been experiencing during that time and my inexperience attempt of cleansing the company's location. We felt so comfortable during the reading and so impressed with his gift of being a medium and knew he was the real deal. Hector gave us instructions on how to spiritually cleanse our home and our auras. After doing his recommendations of the baths with natural products, we noticed the difference immediately. Things at home were back to normal and the negative, heavy energy lingering around us had vanished literally overnight.

The following weekend after our reading with Hector, he came to the business and cleansed it. In less than a week from the cleansing, old clients returned along with new clients. From the first week of September until now February 2014, business has boomed. The profit the business generated was enough to catch up on past debt during the previous slow months and carry a surplus in the hundreds of thousands to close out the year. Hector's spiritual advice and recommendations truly worked. What hector did for us is a blessing to our family and my partners business. We are forever grateful to him and what he does.

Sincerely

Sky From Miami, FL

Chapter 4
Healing Ways

What do we want more than anything else, to be happy, many ways to achieve this one goal with multiple layers. I always think if we are healthy physically and spiritually the rest will fall into place. For example society is overwhelmed with losing weight, not all of us fit the structure or panel we are supposed to be in. There is no way a person who is 5' 5" and thick boned structure can fit the package weight wise of the same person who is small or thin boned so with this in mind we will work on happy but within our type of life. I personally like exercise as a one stop for all our needs, if we are fit the odds are in our favor; with this in mind remember this, anything in exes can have its draw backs, for example some believe as I do that extreme exercise of any type can slow down our quick response as our body goes into a mode fit for whatever we are pushing it towards. This goes for all types of exercise so let's say we are biking, pushing ourselves to the limit can also limit our response times. If we are going on the street this could be hazardous, if lifting and later driving your time to respond to unexpected situations could be diminished fractions of seconds making the difference between skirting and hitting another vehicle or being hit by one.

I'm a believer in steady growth, if you exercise light to medium 3 to four times a week it should be enough. If possible morning is best as this will drive you the rest of the day with plenty of energy. I always suggest taking 3 sublingual vitamin B12 pills, for those of you who don't know those are the ones that dissolve under the tongue. Take one in the morning, lunch and afternoon; your energy level will no longer do the rollercoaster ride throughout the day. Let's try and live stress free in this world, I know this can be difficult. I like going to the comedy club to laugh my issues or concerns away, to disconnect. You can do this in everyday life, diffuse with laughter; blow out the tension with a joke or something sexy.

Come on who does not like a complement, I look at my wife and find her very attractive so I let her know. Especially during stressful situations, if you have the time follow it up with some quality intimate time. In any case laugh a little and the world will seem a better place, try what you did as adolescents, whisper or keep your tone down during an argument. Realize that as the voices go higher and higher pitched so does the heat of the moment. I don't care what you tell me quarreling never solves anything, discuss things when appropriate and keep it between you both; do not draw on past issues keep it clean and it will clean up nicely. Look up old happy moment photos, anything to bring the moment from escalating. Stop stressing, remember your blessings, respond well to situations; stop adding up your troubles and start counting your blessings. This is a simple way to get ready and do what you have to do, from a place of peace, a place of love, a place where you can harness what you need and do what has to be done for anything you desire. My daughter is one that works like this, when she stresses cleaning up her room gives her structure and control so I know she is stressed because she cleans up and organizes the room. Another simple but effective tool to keep you upbeat when you feel foggy is simply grab your feet and as you see your favorite TV show massage your toes. Believe it or not most of the time women go get their manicure, pedicure they are also making themselves feel better from the toe massage they are being given. If you have doubt do it, take a couple of minutes per toe and see what happens.

A secret to lasting in your relationship flip the M in ME. Remember If together does not inspire you to be better, you're with the wrong person because no one can change a person but the right someone can be the catalyst for the person to change for the better. If you don't walk away with any other detail remember, 10% is what happens, the other 90% is what you do with it. Same with conflicts, 10% is difference of opinion, 90% just the tone of your voice so tone it down and soon it will be a distant memory. No matter the situation, silence and smiling are winners, followed by I'm sorry, it's my fault, oh yea how can I fix it are all keys to getting past misunderstandings. Don't compare, don't hold back, give what you can, be nice on the way up the ladder of success, you may meet and need them on the way down; that's right, life has ups and down, feel good about who you are, speak your truth, keep in mind resentment and regret are the true enemies!

Sex is a taboo, maybe in some homes not in mine; we think a healthy sex life can go a long way towards a relaxing life style. For example for most couples morning sex is not the best mostly for women it triggers better in the later hours for us guys anytime is a good time what a surprise. So guys keep it relaxed and you might gain a quality morning or two during the month. Sultry moments for women happen best in the twilight hours, we are not talking of a stolen moment of romance from a new relationship, I'm speaking to you about a long and mature relationship, it needs work to keep it existing. Well if you know what I'm talking about then you are the person I'm addressing in this situation. After years of the same couple we must do all to keep it fresh and if there is love there is always possibility. If we are stressed and not rested who has energy for intimacy so get your sleep, at the very least 7 hours a night should be the norm. I see so many young people not getting enough rest, try 9 to 10 hours until you reach adulthood.

Fantasize, visualize what you are going to do and for goodness sake stay away from alcohol, never a good thing before those private moments. If in the morning, have a quick shower, brush teeth and give yourself some visual moments, as you try to get your erotic mood in full swing. Girls stay away from questions, we guys like to simmer before we are ready to talk about our problems and all you will do is give him a reason to argue about something else, keeping what he's not ready to talk about from being discovered or brought out into the light of conversation. Oh yea if you are with the right person and intimacy is great don't throw it out for obscure and unsure reasons. Figure out what's happening to cause you to feel less attracted to them at other times. Maybe the kids maybe the family maybe they are not the best communicators, shy at other times figure it out because good intimacy can be hard to come by. I would say it's the fountain of youth, for men it can clean up the prostate for women it's a destressor and increased feelings of self-worth by feeling desired and wanted. Remember living without love is like plants living without sunshine, sooner or later they wither and so can we. Remember, a dream only you can see is the dream to happiness, no amount of money can gain you happiness if you're not in a happy place! I would offer an idea, take some time at night and sit on your favorite swing or sun chair; just look up at the heavens, that's right stargaze at the universe at the moon and let your mind soar, your soul rejoice at the wonder of it all. Scan the heavens with your mind, night dream of those heavenly bodies until you forget for a bit any earthbound issues. Just another thought on aligning yourself with the bigger picture of your life; often when we look at how large everything is and how small our little part is we can realize and put into perspective how insignificant the different moments that could down us are and overcome without having a meltdown.

It's not all about couples, how about those looking for love, I'm sure there are quite a few of you out there and I'm not about to let you feel left out. The key is self-esteem; if you feel good about yourself you own the situation. If not there are things and technics that can help. I like acupuncture, find a good one in your area and hit all the depression, anxiety points and look into cooking down that internal heat that throws you into a deep down. Exercise is key, morning is best; keep it to no less than four days a week with one hour of cardio and twenty minutes of weights or other strength building exercises. Touch is essential, if you are touched and they make your skin crawl, then perhaps this is not the right person. If on the other hand it makes you nervous or your heart starts to run wild you've got chemistry.

It's fun when a smell attracts you to another person, some women get down on the monthly visitor but others make them feel aroused, when you kiss just the saliva swapped can be a turn on. Look for signals, body language can make it or break it, if you are sending out the wrong signals then what. Try and look around who looks right, sometimes it's that simple. Think about this concept, we should all have a self-relationship, everyone should before anyone else, this is why I can love deeply and allow myself to be loved the same. It's an age old idea that has never been more applicable than in today's fast paced and disconnected life style. Your feelings, never be shameful to follow them for your happiness, the most unhappy people are the ones who worry about what others think! Do it your way, be yourself, never base your happiness on other's opinions and expectations, this way no one can ever tell you "YOU'RE DOING IT WRONG"!

I can make anyone do my bidding, ok maybe not like that but you can move as the person moves, don't mimic every move but if you are talking to someone observe, they might switch crossed legs, do it in the same direction but not every time keep it to 33% or less. Listen to how they speak if they use particular words like incredible to describe something often try to incorporate some of the common words into your vocabulary. Subliminal commonalities work; Speaking to your supervisor, keep eye contact, don't become a stalker, just long enough to make a connection, as a minimum I suggest 10 seconds no more than 25 or 30 or you might seem desperate or weird. Practice makes perfect, a tendency to slap their thighs then you go ahead, if they do it six times you can do it twice and be safe. You get the idea keep it real, if they use certain words in their writing more often try to incorporate into your reply at least some once or twice. Intimacy is important, let your hair down and talk about something personal enough so you are comfortable and they feel you are sharing.

It's a lie, when you are told you should not share about who you are, you are special and showing or telling others is only a good thing. Envious people might not feel that way but if they do maybe they should not be around you. Maybe you are a good cook, show off with a wonderful meal, and let them know how you got your promotion over all the other people who were in line. Talk about your past successes, maybe you were a teacher for years and you are recalling how much you enjoyed changing the lives of others for the better. If complemented thank them, let them know how wonderful you felt by it. Everything in measure, don't own the room for the night talking about yourself, ask others keep it real after all you want to get to know them as much as they do you. If they touch your soul more intensely than your body, they are keepers, if the timing is not for today, wait for timing is everything in life!

Have you heard of Turmeric, very nice natural anti-inflammatory, yet another tool to keep your gut up to par with the rest of your instrument. This simple spice can help heal another very troublesome area of the human condition, stress. So you can sprinkle powder in your food if you don't like, then you can mix with any other. I like the pill, as you will take it every day; remember even depression, anxiety can be alleviated by using this wonder drug. Give your fingers and toes a massage for at least two to three minutes and reap the benefits of boosting your energy, also stretch your arms out from your shoulders as a windmill. Swing them along with your body front to back for at least one to two minutes. You know how they say something warm will soothe the savage beast, if you wake up in a funk or just any time, just take a big cup of coffee, use a container that lets you feel it's warmth. Just hold it and smell the nice hot coffee, you don't even need to drink it; just let the warm feeling and smell takes that down feeling away. This technique will work with tea as well so the key is just to hold something hot so your hands feel the warmth and your nose can smell the comfort food.

My favorite quick fix is the ice bath, with this in mind try it if you are not pregnant, great if you want to get pregnant but try to stay away from this bath right after a meal. Here is how to do it, a regular bath tub, fill with cold tap water, strip and back into it, your butt lands in the tub and your legs are hanging out the sides, your back against the wall. The key is only that midsection gets wet, so in a full tub of water when your butt is in there only that portion. If you are a woman and have big breasts please use a bra so they do not get wet. Once in stay there 2 to 3 minutes then a loved one or friend must add 6 big bags of ice into this water. Sorry but you must stay 15 to 20 minutes then as you exit you must dry from your feet up so only area that got wet is your midsection. There are tons of probiotics out there, I prefer the natural ones that you must keep refrigerated, only because in its natural state and not dried as in pill form. The pill form is good just rotate the manufacturers not all have the same probiotics and you don't want to miss out on the one that you are in need of.

Bottom line, many ways a person can suffer a health problem, the one stop solution for all is exercise. I've been asked if a small daily dose of aspirin a day can help, the answer is yes, but you should consult with your doctor as there are some medicines that can be problematic if a daily regimen of aspirin is part of your routine. Don't just think heat attach; I would say maybe even half of all the strokes have a high blood pressure component so yes the one small dose of aspirin a day may liquefy the blood and prevent a heart attack or stroke. So do speak to your health professional and if indicated do take this old, tried and proven wonder drug called aspirin.

I want to go back to the business of spirituality, never forget if the body is healthy the spirit thrives, if we are unhealthy the spirit can only perform as strongly as the body is healthy. Again stay healthy it's not just for physical quality of life but spiritual quality of life as well; so you have your hands full to get your whole life healthy not just the physical but the spiritual and they are very similar, the things you must do.   I've included sections on health on both my previous books, Life & Beyond and Light and the Darkness; I've gotten many emails about this topic. I can tell you that although we are a spirit with a temporary body if the body does not function well neither does the spirit. So please take these areas relating to health as a necessary part of spirituality. Remember, living once is enough when done right, concentrate on the moment, not the past or the future because tomorrow will be here soon enough and yesterday's lesson made your todays better!

I've looked at many people with health issues and there has always been a spiritual component. Some come from previous lives others from self-inflicted damage in their current existence. In either case there is always hope to at least better the condition through understanding and spiritual work. By this I mean you can clean the energy and work with hypnotherapy to find where the root of the decease started to close that door to further physical manifestation do to something you were carrying with you from the past. I'm currently working with a woman who had so many things wrong with her but it all stemmed from some emotional damage from the past. She in her youth had a period where she served as an escort, although full of life she diminished herself and her parental teachings so at some level she was at the very least suffering some guilt from what subconsciously she believed to have been doing wrong to herself, her body her spirit.

This manifested in breast cancer, although she was able to cure it without traditional medicine she had a relapse in the ovarian area several years later. All these injuries had to do with the areas she sold for money. She quickly gained weight and began to get more and more depressed. The first time we began a regimen of energy cleansings and I again sent her to a hypnotherapist friend of mine to work on the mental aspect of the disease. Knowing is half the battle, and she was in agreement that it stemmed like the previous time from something in her past. After it was discovered that even earlier in her life her uncle had molested her she got better and the cancer disappeared. There was alternative medicine involved with a mega dose of vitamin c and oxygenated I.V.s along with other treatments to quench the spread of the decease. I'm a firm believer that cancer is a virus and it can only thrive in an acid constitution so keep it neutral or more on the alkaline and no matter the virus it will not flourish.

Meditation and visualization are key ingredients, remember you are what you think and believe. That's how this particular person got into trouble; at some level she began a sub-conscience campaign to self-destruction. Once we beat down the reason for the cause it was just a matter of reversing the damage being caused. I believe that this is why some folks get better quickly and some don't. Once the mindset is on track to heal the body, healing will begin. Get with the program that what you think and believe you can achieve and you will, any doubt and all is flawed, you must believe. No matter the condition if prescription or holistic, read the label or follow the instructions, there are reasons for the limits one can help you one can hurt you so follow prescribed quantities so you may enjoy a healthy solution to your problem or situation. Some if not most holistic is preventive, some say why if I don't need it. In this fast paced world don't get enough of what nature provides so supplements in the right dosage is recommended so you don't need it later medically.

I want to give you a simple guide below that if you follow can help you to better relate with self and others.

How do I feel, look at the words below and identify those who hit home with you, look them up in a dictionary and understand if you were even using the word correctly or if you need to redefine that feeling.

Mad, Sad, Miserable, Jealous, Hurt, Frantic, Ridiculous, Ruined, Alone, Horrible, Empty, Used, Abused, Stupid, nervous, crazy, ignored, ignorant, intimidated, abusive, destroyer, empowered, accused, fearful, unloved, if other words better suit your situations use them but look up the meaning and make sure it fits the circumstance.

Look at the situation you are currently in and identify what you believe is the problem and how the feelings you are experiencing are affecting; how you reason through the problem. In other words what is reality to the problem and what you are bringing in from issues you had and have nothing to do with the situation, stay on talk, don't deviate.

Are you insulting, accusing, are you the aggressor, don't degrade in order to get your point across, after all who's perfect. Are you listening to what they are saying, are you being blinded by your view and are unable to see the big picture, do you feel vengeful, are you making fun of or are being made fun of. Is the situation where you feel hitting is an option, walk away, violence is never the solution, it just opens up another can of worms, escalation to solve a problem is not the answer. Take responsibility for your part in the situation, after all it takes two to make thinks go wrong and it also takes two to find the answer in any altercation. Keep focus on the problem; don't go after the person, rather keep looking for a practical solution to the situation at hand. Listen, open your mind and ears without judgment, respect that person and assume responsibility for your actions in this situation.

Take some timeout and come back to it once you realize if your home has become a war zone. Look, once you realize that things come up and discussing these issues is normal then you can decide if the conflicts are coming up to often. Never resort to violence or attacks as these only worsen situations. Remember pointing fingers also escalates things, put yourself in their place and how would you feel if they were pointing fingers, it would be best if you point at the situation and not the person. It's not about guilt or innocence as it is about solving the problem. Once you hare firmly focused on attacking the particular problem and not the person then look for an amicable solution. Use damage control tactics by healing any bad feelings, sometimes even after a solution is found mending broken fences is part of the healing proses.

Never get into a heated conversation if you are coming from a place of anger, go work out or just take a walk in an air-conditioned mall. Wait for the right time and place to open a dialogue, never point fingers, use an appropriate tone and language, pause and listen to what they have to say keeping an open mind. No matter what stay on task, the biggest hurdle is going of target is never a good thing. There could be more than one way to solve the situation so listen, acknowledge them when there are good points even if you did not come up with it. If the problem is with the children perhaps a mediator, another adult could come in with a fresh perspective. There are no winners or losers, just another potential problem solved!

Look, life is simple if you are predisposed to certain decease make the effort not to let it get the better of your life. Quality living is after all what it's all about so if for example you have a predisposition to high blood pressure because of genetics or other reason than some basics to get you those extra 15 years and not shorten your life by the equivalent. Do your cardiovascular exercises, I don't care what but do them at least 4 times a week, not fifteen minutes but at the very least one hour to get your heart beat up. I guarantee you if you do cardio it will improve your quality of life, not only to protect you from decease but it will increase your libido amongst other areas you will notice improvement. Don't forget certain foods, cantaloupe for example is a good one, so are oranges, many foods can assist in preventing or lowering blood pressure.

Most of us do not know now to properly breathe, so learn to meditate, like any other medicine, in order to achieve long lasting success you must do or use these tools daily. Be at peace, question your inner voice, life is really a blank page, start writing the new chapters, new opportunities stop looking for cracks or kinks in your armor, or flaws in yourself; reach new heights, new potential, greatness lies within. Life is neither beginning or ending, it can be however an excuse to try and get it right in the next 12 months if it's the end of the year, don't reinvent the wheel, everything and everyone around you affords ideas; keep in mind success is inspiration and perspiration together, one without the other is wasted space! I want to recap as I've covered the benefits of exercise throughout this book; the bottom line is with exercise we can live longer, the quality of life will improve as will, sleep, energy, better mood throughout the day, stronger immune system to prevent or fight off any infection and oh yea, stay fit and loose those extra pounds.

 Stress, tiredness, moody, even weight gain can have an emotional component from the past you are not connecting the dots. Come on, you awaken and it hits you, even before getting out of bed, then look back at an earlier time when you felt the same. Don't connect with waking up but with an emotion, look back and remember what you were doing and with who. There could be an emotional component that is causing that high level of procrastination, mistakenly associated with current events. There might be triggers of something similar that is causing this mood shift. Once you make that connection, go even deeper back until you find the last memory that caused the same feeling. Analyze that moment, perhaps it was something at work and now a disconnected situation perhaps with your significant other triggered it incorrectly. You are smart, barring a true need for anti-depressives these techniques will help a large percentage of people that might otherwise fall in the category of pills.

 I want to tell you a personal epiphany when I realized what I say with passion can come to pass; it was during a difficult time for my daughter, her mother had died. I had her back in every supportive way I could even though I had nothing to do with my ex-wife for many years. My only connection to her was our lovely daughter Mary. Not to brag but she is very talented and very mature for her age, she can sing anything and she had won scholarships and awards for this beautiful talent since elementary; please find below her YouTube link as I continue to post new stuff as she has events. I never really had the money to hire a private tutor but she has made it on her own. I've always given her all the moral support and been at all her events and taken her everywhere she has needed to be.

I guess this is often more than money as many who have the monetary support don't have the loving support. In this aspect and all that my means can I support her in this talent. Sorry I took this brief side track but I wanted you to know how much I love and admire my little girl, oh yea you may search her on YouTube as Mary Ellen, or follow the link below. You may also search for her on You Tube by typing Mary Ellen jurame; this is one of the songs she sings and will take you to her channel.

http://www.youtube.com/channel/UCvcQcxP0n2Jafckna2k1UDg/videos

Back to the story it was during the burial day, we had gone to where the priest did his eulogy, wow this guy was too old to be doing this the first three ties he mentioned her name he got it wrong and finally I stood and corrected him. I know maybe not my place as all her family was there. My parents and family had also gone to support my daughter in this time of need. Anyway finally the eulogy was done and I felt I had been out of place but surprisingly all thanked me for my correction. Don't get me wrong most of her family was nice, except for her mother; my daughter's grandmother from the other side was a real piece of work. The grandfather and I got along well and we still do. The aunts are wonderful to Mary especially her aunt and godmother Cristy. As the burial was done, it was weird as her ashes were buried in the ground but hey whatever. As we were walking to our cars Mary left with her mother's family and I was approached by her grandmother. Let me rewind, my dad's health had not been the best and he made his best effort to go so I supported him in his walking through the grass and back to the car. I opened the door to help him in and as I went around the grandmother approached me from the back of the car, she told me that my dad did not look good and he already looked like he had one foot in the grave meaning as we were already in the cemetery and smiled.

I was so furious that the low life former mother in law of mine would stoop at any occasion let alone at a time where they should be grieving to say such nasty things about my dad to me. I just looked at her and said no I believe my dad was fine but I was angry. As she turned away I wished upon her all the bad she could have been thinking about, to befall her but tenfold. Those kinds of wishes only work if the other person is truly thinking or acting in a negative way. So it was within a week she was in intensive care, let's just say she was close to the grave for about three weeks and of course it was not her time so she recuperated.

It was at that moment I realized that I needed to be more careful as to getting angry or making those wishes, especially from a place of anger. Don't get me wrong, she is not a very nice person and through her life she had done lots of wrong to lots of people even to her own family but I know it's not my place to make judgments or to execute these types of sentences. Stop stressing, it's not the anger or what you're going through that makes you happy or unhappy, it's how you think about it; only one person can hurt your happiness, don't count your troubles rather start counting your blessings, you're in charge it was always your choice, choose to be happy!

I hope this story helps those who do as I did to control those wishes and not let the dark side of their nature get the better of them. We all have this duality but part of evolution is to bypass these dark emotions and overcome the human shortcomings we possess. I reflected back to a time where I was in a group of very enlightened people including 2 monks brought from Tibet. We were all giving our bit of knowledge and as we all spoke I was tuned to those two gentlemen who had an aura of peace and tranquility. After the gathering we were speaking amongst ourselves and I gave one of them a message from one of the spirits of his ancestor. He asked me if he could give me message of my own. I was thrilled and said yes; he told me that for me to achieve a higher energy level I must release some of the emotions that often block me from seeing the more subtle energies. I asked to explain he said I must eat less meat and fill my body with more pure energies, in other words eat better and spend more time in meditation. Change is growth, perfection takes small moves, small adjustments, change can bring struggles, draw backs, take responsibility; it's your movie, your dance, follow the rhythms of life or you might become stale and left behind when the music changes and it must, this is life!

I also remembered another time where one of the spirits that accompany me told me in order for him to work with me I must learn to release some of the more earth grounded emotions such as anger or desire. This spirit brings with him the power of life and death, you might ask what this means. Not the power to kill but the power to heal and when possible extend life or rid this inevitable destination for others until their true time is. He explained that many times a person's death is brought on by their actions and not because it is their destiny to pass at that time. But he explained that I must be more pure to properly handle these energies and not abuse the gift. I'm still not there but I hope as I evolve doing this work so I may get to that enlightened place where he might gift me this possibility he brings for me to help others in need.

I've been fortunate to have many people around me I can call friends, some say you can't be friends with the opposite sex, this can sometimes be true but it all depends on your moral fortitude. Just to be on the safe side if you are in a committed relationship, why play with fire after all we are primal and all it takes is time and anyone can slip as you drop your guard with friends from the opposite sex. I was happy on my fiftieth birthday party to have many friends in my home, some from as far back as elementary school.

I have a philosophy of sorts about friendship and it goes something like this, A real friend knows your weaknesses, feels your fears, sees your anxieties, recognizes your disabilities, he knows who you are, understands your past, he knows when to say nothing, when to let it happen and when to pick up the pieces; he gives you freedom to be, room to become without judgment, always calling you friend. Let's face it a real friend is there when in reality sometimes would rather be elsewhere.

Prayer is a very simple way to regain control, remember how much you put into something is how much you will get out of it. So with this in mind if you truly believe if you truly concentrate you may yet achieve a measure of success with prayer. Focus and visualization are critical components for most things. I've been an athlete all my life it was early on that I found that visualization increased my chances to achievement in whatever endeavor I applied myself to. You are what you eat, a very popular saying, well you are what you think even more so; many people go through depressions that are capable of shortening or even eliminating this destructive disease. For those who suffer from it believe me when I tell you it is just as destructive as any other disease so never feel that because it's in the mind it's any less destructive as cancer or aids or any other physical deformity. I like to give a simple tip to get out of the funk, simply bring out some old scrap books and look back at some good memories, before you know it the body gets charged with positive energy and the doom and gloom feeling subsides.

With this being said, a strong mind a focused mind may yet fight off its debilitating effects. I have seen in some of my clients what it can do; I've also seen how it can be turned around once the person finds in themselves the inner strength to overcome with sheer will power. No matter meditation, chanting, or a number of modalities with focus we can achieve a measure of success that is unrivaled with medicine alone. Belief is an essential component, remember you can pray but if all you are doing is reading words there is no power without the emotion, the passion that belief can bring. Life brings inevitable change, awaken and ask, if today was my last day is this what I would do; ask this simple question and if after seven days the answer is no it's time to live, it's time to become the new you, the happy you.

Remember we are like unhatched eggs, we must hatch to become what we must become, if we don't eventually we become as unhatched eggs must, ROTT! I forgot to give this simple remedy, just because I did a cleanse today that reminded me of its curative properties. It's simple Ox Bile, you can look it up on the internet, get the pills, it works with people who get constipated or diarrhea. A no brainer if you happen to be one of those that have problem, no one else knows better than you how well received it will be not to get up and run to the bathroom before an accident occurs.

Feng Shui

I order to find our way in the world we have discovered many modalities that help us navigate obstacles; Feng Shui is one of the most ancient of disciplines that can help us walk on our best path of life. Chi or the flow of energy is how we use this oriental discipline to best navigate through our lives. The flow of energy from all around us can be harnessed and turn a negative flow into a prosperous outcome by realizing it's there and using it or harnessing its power for our benefit. Some of these energies can influence a short period while others can last years. By using this ancient art we can discover when and where and how it applies to our own situations thus maximizing our chances at successfully navigating these flows that exist in our environment.

I want to use this year of the wooden horse as an example of how we can activate or mitigate some of the year's flow, thus creating what can be an abundant flow of positive outcomes for all of us this year. Likewise using some of these examples you can research each of the coming years and benefit from those dates and times that are most beneficial to each of you. In collaboration with your own energy flow you can see the good directions of general energy for the year. For example according to the year of the wooden horse the best energy positions for either home or work environments are South, North, West and South West. What does this mean for you, well if you have a home with a front door in any of the aforementioned position you will have a better chance to have a prosperous year. The key as I've stated before is in activating these points for your particular needs. The negative areas for energy flow this year are East, South East, North West, in other words these are areas to be avoided or not activated. If you are to look at your home and your bedroom is in one of these areas there might be fixes that need to be applied in order to mitigate the negative influences or chi that would be bearing down on those areas.

The areas that I did not mention are mixed and have some favorable and some not so much for the year of the wooden horse, therefore they should be looked at if you are in those areas or if you work in any of these areas. When I say areas you can visualize your home or work place and divide the area into coordinates, north, south, east, west and all the in-between directions. Not all positive flow of energy is good for all directions, you want to have your entrance point to be busy and bring in abundance, however where you sleep you might not want that busy positive energy as this can keep you up at nights thinking up plans to make your billion dollar empire better. You get the notion, positive is positive but not necessarily auspicious for all directions as in the case of the bedroom. If you look at the first book it has a chapter on what are the positive and negative life energies for each year of birth. Although the life energy of the person is important, the yearly energy has significantly more power than a lifetime standard for the person and their year of birth. So we are looking at best for the person to have one of their positive energy positions to be in tune with the year's positive positions. Although yours could be a negative if the position of the year is a positive; I would for that year go for the year's positive as it has more get up and go energy than the lifetime best and worse for the person.

Below is a small diagram that places the numbers to each of the positions for this year 2014. If you recall from my first book I gave the general meaning for each of the numbers so I will briefly recap what can be expected this year for the respective areas. Remember when it comes up Yang areas are busy areas, Air conditioner, Living Room or TV room, Kitchen area, you get the idea while yin areas are basically areas with little or no movements, closets, bathrooms, garages, storage areas in general. By the way, bedroom should be considered a Yin area as most practitioners do not recommend a television, or stereo or office in your bedroom.

S

3	8	1
2	4	6
7	9	5

N

Let's start with the **number three**; located south east and this year could bring arguments and sleepless nights for those who already are susceptible to sleepless nights. The **number eight** usually brings with it good luck, try having a light on 24/7 in that direction or a water feature on the outside of the home to further activate it; open the window that faces south to let all that good luck truly enter your home or work environment. The **number one** also brings with it good fortune and success so on the exterior of this area hand a wind chime, metal would be the correct type; since good fortune is coming to this area find those big dollar coins and string them together and hang them on the wall in that corner use 6 or 9 coins. The **number two** is not a good position, so if you are a rat or already have poor health stay away from this area. For the **number four** or the center of the home I suggest placing a fish tank, make sure it has bubbles in it, to activate romance and a little more concentration for your endeavors of learning. In this area also place something that has mandarin ducks in the area, or any other animals that mate for life to signify your desire to find a life partner if this is your case. The **number six** or west side of the property will help to propel you forwards so it's a good area for office or any other endeavor to push ahead. The **number seven** or northeast side this year can drain you, emotionally, financially and any other way so unless you have no choice stay away from this area. If your door is here protect yourself from robbery as well. **Number nine** or the north area is an area where you should hold off on doing any major renovation, do place a water feature in the area to bring in good luck if it happens to be where your front door is; on a regular basis open a window facing north or the front door to let that good energy engulf the home. The **number five** or northwest is also a negative area this year so keep it quiet, no building and if it can be avoided no sleeping in this area, in either case place some metal objects in that area to diminish it's negative effects. For example you may buy a big metal framed or even metal full metal object and place it right on the northwest wall; also under the bed by the headrest another metal object or a metal bed will do nicely to cancel the negative effects for this year in that area. Placing a big metal wind chime in that corner outside will also do nicely to diminish these effects.

The above numbers will help you if you superimpose them over your home or workspace, and then follow what each means. Remember to always keep in mind your life positions; life positions for the person have nothing to do with the yearly but it does influence. Below also find a wheel that will allow you to find your animal sign as this is done by the year of birth. In order to get a comprehensive chart find a professional as this section is here just to give you a rudimentary idea of Feng Shui and how it can be of help in your understanding of energy flow and the timeliness or untimeliness of your chart.

The Gua number for each of us is essential in Feng Shui; this number does not change for us and is the gateway to many answers and remedies so knowing your Gua number should be your number one priority. We all have some good and some bad positions according to direction and knowing is half the battle; if we choose one of the good ones it maximizes our chances to have a positive outcome or experience, in on the other hand we choose a negative direction it can create havoc in our life path . How do I obtain this Gua number, well it's a calculation based entirely on your year of birth. We have as you will see four good positions and four bad ones so if you follow nothing else try and stay within your four good ones for your front door and bedroom and all will be better in your life. Remember the most important in this day and age is the main bread winner but there are four so as long as you and your significant one are in a good one you are good to go. Statistically speaking if you are with a partner at least two of your good positions will be the same as your partners if not for the same reasons. For example your number one good position might be for abundance and for your partner it might peaceful sleep. So as long as you both have some in common the home will work for both of you even if they are not for the same purpose.

Positive Energy Flow

	1	2	3	4	6	7	8	9
Prosperity/respectability	SE	NE	S	N	W	NW	SW	E
Long life/good-romance	S	NW	SE	E	SW	NE	W	N
Good health/harmony	E	W	N	S	NE	SW	NW	SE
Peace/stability	N	SW	E	SE	NW	W	NE	S

Negative Energy Flow

	1	2	3	4	6	7	8	9
Accidents or injuries/arguments	W	E	SW	NW	SE	N	S	NE
Failed relationships bad-encounters	NW	S	NE	W	N	SE	E	SW
Injury/legal-issues/fire	NE	SE	NW	SW	E	S	N	W
Misfortune/health-concerns/unproductive career	SW	N	W	NE	S	E	SE	NW

No it's not a typo, if you realized it the number five above is not used, that's because the number five is in the center palace and thus does not have a direction. All of you that sit on number five will use as your number the same as those using number two.

There are several ways to use your birthday year and figure out you Ming Gua number:

*First Method:

For men:

Let's use 1964 are an example and always remember no matter what the number is reduce it to a single digit.

Calculate for Men: 1+9+6+4=20 bring it down to a single digit 2+0=2 subtract outcome from 11-2=9 is the Gua number for a male born in 1964

For Women:

Let's choose 1994 as an example,

Calculate for woman: 1+9+9+4= 23 2+3=5 then always add 4 to the single digit resulting number 5+4=9 is the Gua number for a female born in 1994

Let's try this other way and you decide what way works better for you:

*Second Method:

Take the last two digits of the year so for example 1961 you simply use the 61.

For men you would divide by nine 61/9=7 take that number subtract it from 10-7=3 and this is the Gua Number for a man

For a woman take 1994 and add 5 to the last two digits 94+5=99 divide 99/9=0 left over so any 0 left over in the equation for men or women will always go back to 9 is the Gua number.

Now let's look at the same 1994 for a man: 94/9=4 10-4=6 is the Gua number, just so you realize it does not have to be the same for a man and a woman although born on the same year.

To show you that when the outcome is 0 no mater man or woman the Gua number always becomes 9 here is an example: 1976 for woman 76+5=81 81/9=0 left over so the Gua number is 9.

Now that you have a rudimentary idea of Feng Shui let's talk about some of the basic cures when a star is affecting you in a negative manner.

I will group them by elements to make it easier:

1=Water metal activates this star, while water can be used to activate this star, wood is best to cure excessive water star.

2,5,8=Earth Metal cure for 2,5 as 8 is a good star and does not require a cure only activation.

3,4=Wood water can be used to activate star 4, fire can be used to cure star 3, use a lamp or candle but these days bulb are the best just don't use those cold ones use one that gets hot.

6,7=Metal also activates these stars, while a water cure can be used to treat star 7,

9=Fire if you want to cool down fire, use earth in the form of rocks, rocks or similar to lessen the heat of fire.

You get the idea but if you wish to use any of the elements to cure a star you should do it on a day that element is active so for example if you want to cool down fire activate the cure on an earth day. If you want to activate an area of the home and don't have any of the aforementioned cures, try and just putting on music and sing along or dance to the music for a good 20 minutes and it's done. Again in this year of the Wood Horse the elements that are most abundant are wood, fire and earth so to benefit the most this year is the Goat, Tiger and Dog, while the Rat needs to take extra care are is very little support for them from the elements this year. Keep in mind when looking at an individual there is a year, month, day and hour pillar. All are important but to keep what's important for the year I would get the four pillars of your life and focus on the year and day pillars.

I want to cover the year 2014 now from the animal portion of this great study, remember every year there are variations as the numbers rotate positions in your life every year.

Rat

Really more like a chameleon, as they adapt to their situations and surroundings better than any other in the zodiac. Their nature is to succeed, they look at situations and make the best of them without as much as a hiccup.

For this year the rat needs to use more caution than other years, in this year of the wooden horse there will be obstacles especially for the rat who is always ready to more forwards. There will be good times but overall this year the cautionary tale of the rat is caution. As any year with more effort you can still achieve but have no doubt you will have to be at your best to overcome and realize your goals. Unexpected obstacles do not come free as expenses are always going to go up, especially unexpected so conservation and moving forwards but with caution. In love the rat will experience more opportunities than usual if in a relationship do not mix work and home life as your home will be your stability this year. As in any complicated year, stay away from risky physical endeavors as injuries could easily occur. If you feel sick, don't wait visit the doctor right away as this is one of those years those who wait could be too late.

Ox

Hey, this is a year where you can use your God given talents to the test and excel at leadership and helping other through difficult situations. The last few years have been slow but this year will open doors for those who dare and by the time 2015 arrives you will have more than you expect so go forth ox and take a chance. This is a year where hard work will have a bountiful return, don't get stubborn and you will achieve, look at the big picture and don't let setbacks stifle you. Remember to keep an open mind in your personal life, plenty of good advice is coming so just listen and for those single ox opportunities will be no less. For those in committed relationships open your ears and listen to the advice to those close to you as they might have a soft touch to help you through tough times. This year those ox who plan and don't take unnecessary risks will do very well, remember unexpected accidents like climbing a ladder to get to the roof or forgetting to stop at a red light could take luck out of your hands. Be careful with poor digestion and high blood pressure as well as allergies, since I'm an ox I've done some extra with this one and unfortunately things like this could cause unnecessary headaches along the way to 2015. Like most signs the Ox has deficiencies, amongst the most common is their tempers, keep them in check or they might suffer, keep an eye on rest or your endocrine system might suffer.

Tiger

Oh yea, this year unless you become impulsive or aggressive should be one of the better years for this cat. Remain calm, cool, and collected and keep stress and emotional problems away. You could gain the good will of others by showing that you care, no running of the mouth just stay your course and let what at the moment seem as an obstacle might turn out as a great opportunity. In other words don't jump as the cat usually would and instead keep a look and see what happens until you get clarity and this will be a very good year for you. Take care of your back and digestion, do not eat late and if you do physical activity this year by all means stretch before and after to stay limber and avoid back issues. Use wisdom and a low profile, keeping an open eye for suggestions and ideas will set the pace as you go through hard work and the finish line will shine a light on your work and recognition will manifest. Easy does it in amorous situations, no pouncing, rather listen and learn before committing, if in a relationship don't be confrontational rather take the wait and see route this year. One key element to overall success is get your 8 hours of sleep, this feline needs the rest to be clear headed before going on the prowl. This year be careful becoming friendly with someone other than your relationship if you are in one, also be diligent not to drink too much as it can be disastrous.

Rabbit

You timid creature, this year make sure you wear your feelings on the outside and to your close family and friends show the real you. It's time for you not to shy away as your insecurities might guide you to do, so far that has not worked as well as you thought. Attention to detail will get you where you want to go this year, the first few months might be a bit difficult if you are dragging baggage but the obstacles will be removed and then it's up to you to leave it behind and assume this mantle of success that is being offered to you this year. Stay fixed on the ball and you will get all the rewards you have coming, do your ground work and success will arise for you this year. Look at opportunities and realize it's all about you so take it as it comes but don't drop the ball on opportunities to go higher and higher. Listen to the advice of your loved ones keep your communication channels open, and if you're looking for a job pass the word along and you might get all the help you need. This year you will be blessed with heaven luck so if you need help ask and you shall receive; stay working out and blow off any pent up stress, eat right all will be possible for you this year. Be careful in august with an injury and September brings opportunities for new relationships.

Dragon

This year this big hearted creature should be grateful for all that has been done and all that will be done on their behalf. Stay focus on task and don't let distractions get the better of your time. Finish what you start but keep an eye open for opportunities outside the realm of your goals. If someone brings opportunity to your door do not dismiss it, just because it was not in your greater plan; sometimes from nowhere the future could come forth and present alternatives. Better money management is essential this year, if you want to save or pay off on old debts. If in relationships learn to listen and allow the opinions of those you care for to be heard, if single go forth on the work front and along the way you may yet meet that special person. Safety in prevention, so take vitamins make sure you get enough sleep and by all means do not let the ugly head of depression gain a foothold in your life. Complicated year with financial stress, changes to occur midyear if you drink or other vises then be extra careful as it could further complicate an already difficult year.

Snake

Very much the person who can obtain what they desire through charm, when they want to; if you really scrutinize them all will see it's a facade. They are so good at it that unless you are paying close attention you might believe all they have to offer. This year will be a little better than the last but still under pressure to perform the snake will have to be at its best to excel throughout the year. Safety in the sense of not taking chances is important this year so become aware of opportunities but before launching your ship consider all your options carefully. In other words think before you speak is key so you do not start the ball rolling in the wrong direction from nothing it could become an avalanche so eyes open and mouth shut until you are sure. For those looking for love keep nose on the grindstone of work but have a neon light overhead letting the world know you are a pre-owned but certified vehicle ready for the ride of your life. Exercise regularly but exercise caution in every aspect of life or you could end up with emotional and stress related headaches. Get a grip as this will overall be a better year from your previous few; for older and young snakes alike health is something to be careful with.

Horse

Wow, slow down and remember if you were born in a Horse year or day you will like all signs have your ups and down but if you stay true to your work ethics the end product will be a positive one for you this year. A sine wave like those that come out of an oscilloscope will be an accurate depiction of this year with plenty of ups and downs. As most of the downs will be tempered if faced with truthfulness you should navigate the difficult periods by showing your integrity on your chest as you blow down any obstacles with perseverance and honesty. Your support system will widen and all hands will be on board with helping you move forwards, if investing is your thing make sure you do before February 2015. This year you might want to hold off on any major battles in relationships as they may spiral out of control and an eventual depression set in after you reflect and realize it was too much return for what was happening. Find a way to blow off steam at the gym, hit the weights or cardio and be careful with stupid accidents.

Goat

It's okay to be nice but not stupid, so do what you can when you can but letting others take advantage of your good nature is not to be allowed this year. This is your year to reap rewards so if studies is your thing A's will be the answer; if done with school then any project you undertake will have good outcomes but surrounded by envy and jealousy as others see your success. Take this good year to strengthen your self-esteem and don't let distractions side track this year of opportunities so think with your mind and don't make emotional decisions. This is an overall good year and for the girls in this sign you might just land or close escrow on your long relationship, perhaps even marriage will come in before this year is over. Get your head in the game and if things don't seem to be panning out get your energies cleaned as you might be dragging some negative stuff from others and this could be holding you back on this otherwise good year for the goat. Make sure you get enough rest and keep you immune system working at an optimum, do not want you running out of steam. A golden year to obtain your goals so if you have them chase them down if not get with the program and make some so before the year is done you may yet make them a reality.

Monkey

Hectic year so stay focus and don't let the sheer amount of stuff around you this year overwhelm things for you. One step at a time is a key for survival this year, bring to bear all your talents and overcome obstacles you will. I definitely understand if you feel overwhelmed and tend to forget to nurture those closest to you; no matter, stay in the zone and give your loved ones the time they need from you. This type of year can bring some lonely times but that's why we have telephones, if not close reach out and talk until you compose yourself, remember you are not alone. Better communications could mean better relationships, also this year be careful if you don't follow up with the doctor as any simply thing could become a serious health issue.

Rooster

Now here is a character, with all the attributes to get you on their side and the way they can work the room makes them easy to help you forget they can be arrogant. Smooth is their middle name but if you give them enough rope they will entangle themselves so for these roosters the object is to keep level headed and not always believe their own B.S.. Your time is just getting started roosters, if you polish your craft whatever this might be successful you will be over the next two to five years. This is the time to look around and sharpen skills for the future, look at strong women around for help, it could literally mean a female driven industry or product might be your way in to a new business opportunity. Time to find a partner or solidify that relationship; perhaps maybe even marriage is in your cards in the not too distant future. If what you are into is a good thing go with the flow, definitely solidify your positions no matter work or personal.

Dog

Many things have seemed out of reach, not anymore; the time for you to fine tune your talents and start to reap some rewards are here. Unfortunately it might become a bit much in the sense that you could lose perspective and get a bit full of yourself. Yea, you are ready to ascend the ladder of success, so now what? You will see people around you look to you for answers and acknowledge you talents and wisdom, keep in mind that along with success there are those who wield that jealous bone and might want to trick you. Upward motion in your chosen career is key this year and for you, a creative venue is the way. Respect, admiration and all those things you have been looking to attain are coming your way; any distractions must be tempered so you do not lose your way or your opportunities. This is the year to learn to harness your calm demeanor and give yourself good advice, by now you are aware that others are happy with your suggestions but look at the mirror and realize you must give yourself the same quality advice in decision making you do for others. Under all circumstances family is a must to even if you are busy it's time to connect with your roots, those who love and have supported you. Take time and visit the elderly and give them a bit more of your time so they can enjoy your lovely personality. It's a bit hectic but love is definitely in the air; always choose your life path first, at least during these years where growth is afforded to you by the universe. Saver a little for your personal time, after all who does not like to be loved; for now it's all short term attention in the love arena so don't make more of anything as everything is starting to go, go, go for you this year. Insomnia, constipation and just plain tiredness, it's almost too much for you but with good exercise you will balance out. Learn to meditate, acupuncture is also a good thing to keep your nervous system from crashing. Take your vitamins and keep your focus on the ball as this is the beginning of good things to come.

Pig

This person will do well this year as they evolve into a higher level of management and leadership. Those with their noses to the grindstone will be able to give to others by sharing in their good fortune. Although they tend to be even a little gullible to the point of being taken advantage of the realization of their dreams in a competitive environment will invigorate them to reach new heights. Down side is simple don't go beyond the point where you will be so tired that enjoyment of this new found good fortune is unattainable. So take a breath and make sure you rest and as you are the easiest to get along with in your group so should you enjoy and rejoice in this wave of good luck that if done well most pigs will enjoy this year. Get together with trusted friends and coworkers so all may enjoy and reap the long term rewards. Don't be disappointed if the rewards come slowly it's a ladder that not all climb at the same speed but be assured that those pigs that work it will achieve all they aim for. Drink plenty of fluids and find a balance between success and quality time with those you love and the expansion time for you will not stop this year.

An analysis of the four pillars is also an essential for a complete analysis this portion of Feng Shui will give you a more detailed view of your year, month, day and time of birth. In order to get the big picture this is a must part as it will show how timely your sign will be according to when you were born and the element associated with your sign. Most people talk about the animal sign but there is an animal sign assigned to your hour, day and month as well. In order to see the complete picture calculating the four pillars will give you the animal sign and element that the rest of your chart works with. For example the year 2014 is the year of the wood horse but if you knew your day animal and element this might show you a much broader canvas of what is expected this year for you. If you are a rat day there is work to be done to mitigate the downside that is coming for the rat this year. If on the other hand you are pig or sheep for the day of your four pillars then the odds are you will be experiencing a seamless year. A good day will boost your chances to going through a year with mostly up times.

I'm constantly asked about western astrology and how it compares to Chinese astrology, the comparison is not equal as western astrology is based on planetary alignments and this one is more considered based on blocks of time and the 10,000 year Chinese almanac. The twelve animals and the five elements are the foundation of how to dissect or analyze your destiny. Remember each of the four pillars is assigned an animal and one of five elements, how they work together can show you having a strong or weak chart. In Chinese astrology what is looked for is balance, for all the different animals and elements to be in balance or harmony. Too much of any one animal or element could throw things off or make it dominant and what we want is balance. As in life if we have just the right amount of each part of your personality then we flow too much of anything is generally not a good thing. No matter what form of divination used it is based on the assumption of probability, if you have a strong chart the probability is you will have a good life. As with most forms of divination this can be brought down to the day and hour of the day. However the broader the time frame being looked at the better the probability you will be affected by the energies calculated to rule you for those dates.

Chapter 5
Dream Visions

I've been experiencing visions as waking messages and dreams for weeks now; no one knows of them as of yet. I have to put into some semblance of order or at the very least understand what is real and what part of the jumble that occurs during dreaming. I've received many waking messages; some are so wild that I've been hesitant to speak of them even to the family. I'm now ready because I decided that if I can't make heads or tail on my own maybe writing about it will offer me a different perspective; maybe I'll remember something from some of them that will finally begin to make sense. After all who's to say dreams and nightmares are not as real as reality, so I will allow some wiggle room until I can prove or disprove it. If it can exist in your mind it has a chance for reality. I will write this chapter as it happens so if it seems out of context or time bear with me.

It all started one night, I had a strange person come into my dream and explain that I was going to be recruited to help with an ongoing scenario occurring worldwide. He gave me a speech "all it takes for evil to win is for a few good men and women to do nothing", at the time I thought what a crock. After several other visions I decided to start focusing and asking my own guides what it was all about. I get a lot of random stuff in my life so I don't always pay the messages mind.

Remember with what I do sometimes our dreams are just a way to make sense of the days happenings. If you're having trouble at work your dreams could easily reflect work related scenarios. Well I deal with many different people and some of the things that they are going through can manifest as dreams to me in attempts to proses some of the weirdness.

Let's get down to the problem, I've been visited over the last month or so by many strange beings; by strange I mean I've never seen them before they are not part of my regular group of spirits. These spirits seem more like recruiters; you know the ones that want to sell you an idea, a concept or ideology. I'm always a bit hesitant for anyone to sell me a bill of goods so it's no different at the spiritual level. Everyone has an agenda and in that realm it's no different. I'm reflecting back to one of my earlier encounters when I was taken to a place where good and evil meet to iron out their differences. The carnage was horrific and I recall how one of those beings came to tell my protector who had taken me how they felt that place was not for me and I should be taken back to my earthly realm.

I also remember on another occasion when I channeled an angel who had gotten lost on this our earthly plane, how after years of wondering without connecting with above it channeled through me to regain enough strength to reach upstairs or heaven and call home as it were. So I know things are in turmoil with the folks above; I know because of the angel but what it all has to do with me is perplexing. I started with messages through dreams, most are very similar, most require me to do something or join something, and in any case I have to become part or become active at a certain level I've not encountered before.

It was after these dreams became waking, I realized that it was not a pipe dream on my part. With all the movies and other media going on about spirits and other realms I attributed some of this stuff as acting out those fantasies as part of my dream fantasies. Believe me I spend enough time doing this for real not to want to do it in my dreams or any other state. So again when I started getting messages while awake; this was occurring to me not at any particular time or place, it seemed random. I've been eating with my wife, driving to see my parents, speaking with the kids so there is no one trigger I decided to stop ignoring and pay close attention. Reality is a persistent illusion we live in, thank goodness for those fantasy moments to help us escape, so what exactly is going on I keep asking myself. Am I losing my grip or is this something new being brought to my plate; as I explore I feel grounded and stress is status quo so I will continue to focus until I get clarity.

I thought it would bring me clarity to focus on what was being told to me but instead it became more surreal than ever. I don't have any friends that can help as no one I know has ever spoken of these types of messages. The reality is that I have my niche; I work cleaning dirt from the living and give messages from beyond. So when I'm being told that there is more to what I was being shown that I could ever imagine I started to worry. The message was simple, there are groups of dark souls living and otherwise that are attempting to corrupt our very existence and I'm being asked to join the other side. The side that maintains the balance, this made me flash back again that time where I was taken to the battle ground between good and evil. I was told that good does not want to win the battle but to maintain the balance or the stalemate.

I understood the concept, it's a lot easier to keep balance than to try and win so I understood how important it was to throw off the waves of negative energies attempting to corrupt our existence from those dark walkers. Again I thought if things were so balanced why I was being recruited to help, after all I'm low man on the totem pole of spirituality. What I mean by that is I'm living and not a spirit without a body, so my view is very limited to what I'm shown. My belief is when our soul chooses to live this life it gets wiped of all memories from previous lives. You know how hard it is to live this life, imagine with all the experiences from previous lives. When we pass that vale as our bodies die, we are opened up to all those other lives and then and only then do we realize why the things we went through had to happen.

Don't get me wrong, at every encounter they made it clear that it was a choice but how do you say no when you have a family and knowing what I know the realization of the harm that negative energy could easily affect them just like any other person living this existence. What a dilemma and I still have no answer as to why this was happening and why me. I tried to narrow down my focus by type of entity but they were not always the same nor were they from the same realm. What I mean is some were souls others were other things like angels and yet some undefined energies I have no knowledge of what they are. All I can tell you they were all creatures of light, I can feel the goodness but also the urgency of their plead. From my last book Light and the darkness where I detail all the spirits I work with one is from another world not earth I know all this is possible.

Remember there is no time upstairs so urgent to them could mean years to us or it could mean it's already happening, whatever this is and they are simply recruiting more for the continued conflict. All kinds of ideas flooded in, are we loosing and maybe I'm some replacement; I would think when this was set in motion, they had all they needed. That angel story I briefly told came to mind if an angel prepared was sent to this planet and could have been so trashed that it lost its way what can I possibly do to help such a situation or engagement. I recall my teachings where in the past my own entities have told me how we do our part. They told me we are but specs of light on a Christmas tree, one does not do much but place all the lights and it's beautiful and covers the tree lighting up the entire canvas. So much to digest and I'm still not sure what exactly they want from me and why. Really why is the big question, of all the souls why me?

On one occasion, this was a waking dream while I was sitting at the sofa with my wife; we were watching one of her favorite shows, so it was not even something that made me think of anything of this kind. I like Sci-Fi and she likes romance so it was a tear jerker type of show; the spirit came as I was with her and took me to a place where we talked what seemed hours. Yea right, it was but minutes, anyway while there he sat me down and explained that there were options and the first was to say no; I asked what options; mistake number one I should have taken the easy way out. Not knowing where this was headed I thought it could be relevant to my family so I never considered the alternative that was to follow. What was detailed to me seemed surreal but all this information was not something from my own mind as it was foreign to me even while I was experiencing it.

It's been about two months now and the visits have become more frequent, not only during my dream hours but also awake during the day. I found there is no specific time or situation they just come and it's like time stops. I had one time that I was taken to this place for what seems like hours and when I returned my wife asked, were they talking to you, I just told her yes. I realized it had been no more than a couple of minutes at most in what we call the real world. Who's to know what is real and what is not, I can't believe I'm even considering that. Wow, I must be going out of my mind but the times I'm taken seem just as real now as the time or life I spend here.

I'll give you one example so you get the idea, I was just sitting in the sofa, we had just finished diner and were going to enjoy a movie I had rented when it happened. Before I realized it I was at another place; this time it was a group of people and some energies that I don't have a clear word to describe except ethereal. Yea, like a cloud of smoke or energy, no matter always one or more come to greet me and start to talk to me about how things are on earth. I took control and asked why I was being brought to that place, another energy just manifested and turned into a woman. She approached and the others looked at her, I guess the look and feel of her was for my benefit. In either case she asked me to sit down, the scene looked like a movie, the landscape was of Ireland, if you have seen it hills and rock country side. Very pretty, a sunny day I would say mid-day as I could feel the sun above us, anyway she approached asked me to sit and she began to diagram a scenario that to me was head scratching and mind boggling.

She told me a story as old as time, interesting choice of words as she explained that in that form or that place we could travel back and forth in time. Not only to view but to act upon circumstances. I said, "Time travel" not as you understand it she answered but compress time more like it. This is why when you return to your earthly life it seems like seconds or minutes have passed. She asked surprised "you have experienced this reality before" I said if you mean that time one of my spirits took me to that place of giants where a huge battle was taking place. She smiled and said exactly, that moment you experienced happened many thousands of years before. You were given a gift to see how the universe works, checks and balance is how things are kept in order.

She explained there are elements that want to speed up the proses but existence cannot be rushed it must move forward as quickly or slowly as the slowest evolution of the being. If we were to allow this tampering she said the natural order of evolution would not work and a very skewed version of what was to be would occur. She explained that their job was just to let evolution occur naturally without interference from any factions who feel they know better. I reflected back to that alien spirit that works with me, he showed me how old the universe is and many life forms are very old and some not so much like us. I'm not sure from what I could comprehend it seems they have learned how to navigate the time line by simply stepping off at any point; not sure if what they showed me is a recreation that we can see but not change anything or true time travel.

She explained there is a plan set in motion since the beginning of time and even beyond that. Even they were not there at the beginning but as time unfolded certain beings evolved past their primitive existence and were called to serve the greater good. We call them angels she said. There are many other beings higher and lower on the totem pole of evolution and not all are in accord with what has been set as the status quo or natural evolution. It is these elements we try by various means to prevent from modifying what is to come. I asked you mean evil, she explained that is a word developed to differentiate one side from another. Corruption is what they call it, corruption of the time line of natural evolution of souls or species. In either case from time to time that other side as we call it attempts to use lower energies such as ours to gain a foothold on the great plan.

Have you discovered or just detected reality; I just did, even thought you might change down to the core, your beliefs, your values, maybe self-exploration, don't ignore such feelings, grow to understand, to explore new horizons. I'm learning that everything changes, much more so as we read about the unknown, enlightenment of our surroundings is an eye opener, all you have to do is be open to new ideas, concepts, the possibility of others being right, of you being wrong and oh boy I'm I having my eyes opened with this experience. I believe the goal in life isn't to live forever it's to create a reality that will; all things come to pass and so must we. So with this new or renewed focus I go forth into this new understanding of reality.

Back to my story, so the good side as we call it makes an equivalent strike in the other direction in attempts to stabilize this incursion. I get it, it's like I'm being recruited by them to keep their order on earth. She answered correct, she explained how free will is key at our level of existence growth and evolution is key so no matter we are given the option to choose. She told me I can select people to help me as she said I have met some people that have capability and it would be my choice who to pick in the endeavor. One thing she explained it must be in groups of 7, 11, or 17 the quantity of people I choose. If I choose not to involve any people I know then I would be offered the opportunity to join a group being put together by another. I asked how would I know, she smiled and said don't worry you will be approached and with the level of knowledge we have given you it will be easy to understand what they are talking about.

Again, this time I returned and it seemed like seconds have passed, my wife again asked if they were talking to me. You must understand I try and act as if nothing, who wants to be around someone who talks to no one so I've learned to do what I do without any but the most minimal of gestures for only someone like my wife who knows would become aware and even she sometimes does not catch that I'm getting a message. It's funny on this day before the movie was over I took another unexpected trip. The energy or being was different the scene was more up in the clouds and not as easily deciphered. He explained that not all beings involved in this situation were from my planet as this was a universal push and not just my little world. He hopes the way he is manifesting is not distracting but where he comes from is very different than where I'm from. I asked about the spirit that channels through me from another world, he explained that they are aware of that world and although very evolved they still could suffer the same fate as the rest of the universe if not protected. He said evolution shows them how that particular world is close to ascending or an evolutionary growth to take their place amongst the next level of beings. However until that moment or tipping point they are still vulnerable to these lower level attacks.

It's been a few days but no communications from those energies; I guess they are waiting for me to make up my mind of what to do. Remember there is always free will; it's not orders we must choose to do or not do. I spoke with several spirits that I work with about this issue or offer if you can call it that. The feedback I got is, I'm doing enough with what I'm doing here on planet earth and if I choose to do this the world will become a much bigger place but the risks to my existence will also multiply. I asked what they were talking about, they explained that at that level my soul could be lost at least dislodged from my body and if that happens while on one of these trips my body would die.

What to do, I can't simply say no, the offer is at the very least exiting, after all this is what I do here to a much lesser degree. At the very least this would be an adventure not just for me but for my souls evolution I would think. What to do, I'm at a cross roads, initially this was just a weird meeting with new energies or souls but after all these conversations I'm beginning to see how important this could be. I could say there are others probably better suited to the task but yet I was approached so maybe they saw something in me I've yet to discover. Maybe this is what my spirits had been telling me about a new spirit coming in to work with me. No, it can't be these are not souls coming to assist me in my work here they are asking me to assist them at a much broader scope of endeavor.

Well I just hit another milestone; I was taken again and shown the devastation that these souls with an agenda different to the common good to the evolution of a species caused. I was taken to a place where many different souls lived, I say lived because there had been some sort of catastrophe of unnatural nature. They explained over a century had passed since this planet had experienced that up evil that is poised to happen to several worlds now. I guess now in their term can be in another hundred years or it could be tomorrow. They do not see time as we do nor do they experience time as we do; I have deduced this from their visits, by the way they have communicated with me so far. Remember every time they have taken me it's been seconds or minutes in our time but my experiences have been hours even days on some occasions. This trip I just took I can tell you must have been several days but by my clock I was only gone for two to three minutes. So in a blink of an eye in eternity an entire world could be taken to the brink and lost from the path of evolution. I wonder what happens to all those souls when an entire species dies out; is it like a war with us when hundreds of thousands of souls are lost in battle. All I can say even after 100 years that world still looked baron; they must have experienced some sort of major catastrophe because nothing green or living was growing over the surface of the planet I was taken to.

I'm having some sleepless nights thinking about this situation, as I look at the clock it's 3:30am and I'm in front of the computer. I'm grappling with a choice that for once in my life has me at a cross roads. I've been in the military and spent my life as a competitor in a variety of disciplines, judo, jujitsu, gymnastics, dancing, boxing, and others always a competitor, I even became world champion as an arm-wrestler representing the Unites states. I'm no stranger to challenge and overcoming obstacles to achieve a goal, this is no different, is how I have to look at the situation. I can't be overcome with doubt, there must be a reason I've been approached. I can't help the feeling I might not be up to the task. I've strengthen my mind and well my body is a bit out of shape but I feel strong with my soul; is it enough, I guess someone thinks so, I'm having doubts. I'm sorry I like to hop but I just remembered how I overcame a time where some insomnia set in; if you recall at least once you ate late and had a restless night. It's not just you but all of us have a finite amount of energy and unfortunately the body uses the most to digest food. If you are sleeping or just in bed the body needs to work harder digesting a late meal than if it were the middle of the day and your body movements were helping with the digestion. So with this I say no late or large meals as the last of the day.

Remember when you were little and your parents put you to bed at the same time or you have done for your kids. The best adjustment for the body is repetition, if you go to bed at l0pm for example no matter if tired or not, no matter if sleepy or not, you hit that pillow and lay there until to sleep you go. No matter how difficult if you stick to this routine your body will remember. Come on no TV or music or books or lights on, as a matter of fact until you got it lower the temperature to at least 70 degrees; about the only activity you can do with a reasonable chance to still go to sleep at night is sex. I admire my daughter's capability for sleep, she can do anything including exercise at night and come home shower and right to bed she goes. That brings me to the next problem for insomniacs, no exercise of any kinds after 5pm. That's right exercise in the morning or weekends but nothing late or you will be wide awake as if you've had two pots of coffee. So I hope coffee or any form of caffeine is off the table as it will definitely cause you to stay up. I'm sure you are not alone and there are others around you that have had or are having this problem, talk about it perhaps they have the answer to your specific sleepless nights.

Ok, sorry, back to my situation, some of the visions are wide awake, some are while I'm asleep; this last one was about 4:30am as I glanced at the clock when I returned and woke up from the experience. I asked if I can join on a trial basis, they explained that my path of life will be shifted and my entire destiny for this life will be redirected so the answer was no. It's a choice and once in it I'm to take my life my soul completely out of the purpose I'm in and put all my efforts into this new life. They explained I would still do what I do but on a regular basis I would have to travel and encounters with very dark energies will be common so I must choose carefully. I asked if my spirits will be with me, they said some will but others will choose to stay and work their own path on the earthly path. Again I anguished about this decision, what to do, there is really no one to talk to about this, no frame of reference to consider my options.

I had some issues within the family that made me consider doing this, perhaps an escape but after cooling down I realized that whatever the issues I was needed here and life without me at the family level would be financially disastrous. Yes, I'm like everybody else with issues and feelings. This sometimes becomes a difficult thing to manage as I'm expected to be more, but thanks to God I'm able to take myself out of the equation and resolve my work without letting my personal life get in the way. For the most I live a very relaxed life and we just had a gratitude party at my home about a week ago where over fifty of our family and friends came to partake in gratitude for all life has given us. It's healthy to realize and appreciate all we have and stop looking at what we don't. We lose site that things can always be worse as we look at others and their misfortune we realize how good we have it; even though like anyone we have little issues. Even those are part of the proses of growth and some of the things that happen no matter how impactful with time we realize it was to move us on.

Today I was sitting in my backyard, I was in my sanctuary where I like to sit and meditate when I need clarity; it was about 10pm when I decided to sit and meditate. Please find below a picture of my special place where I can relax and reflect. I awoke from my meditation, I was directing it to my dilemma of this quest I've been offered when I opened my eyes I had a butterfly on my right knee and a moth on my left. I did not move I simply took a few minutes to see if there was a meaning, I could not find one. I'm sure amongst my readers there are some whom have knowledge of both animals and might give me some clarity as I did not understand the meaning. Hey, I don't claim to know more than I do and this was outside the scope of my knowledge. I looked and found two pictures that represent the two that I clearly saw on my knees before they just flew away. You can go on my web site, www.heaven2earth.info or hector@heaven2earth.info to send me some ideas if you would be so kind.

On a broad canvas meaning, usually if you refer to the right, the meaning is the mainstream or the accepted ideology and on the left side generally speaks of those in opposition to the mainstream. If you were to look at it from a political view the right side of the house and the left; traditionally the right is where the mainstream of the political climate and the left side is the opposition to whatever the right side stands for. In the theological view those on the right represent on the side of God and those on the left are the ones that oppose the teachings of God or the gospel. Not sure if this is how I should interpret, and thus my question of the meaning. Remember spirituality is a science so question all and if it sounds right then more than likely it is, but if you have any doubt question and question some more until it's true meaning becomes clear to you or in this case me. For those of you that have been cleaned spiritually if you recall on more than one occasion perhaps the person cleaning you would say I'm cleaning the left side and the explanation was that there is where the concentration of negative energies or spirits would be found has the same foundation as I've just explained.

The above are examples I found of the animals on each of my knees, the butterfly on my right knee and the moth on my left if that had a significance I don't know as well but there they were. Maybe the moth was a possibility at night but not the butterfly and both landing on equivalent parts of my body at the same time and when I was meditating, curious to say the least.

Again I was doing some relaxing after a busy day of clearings and readings and once again something strange occurred, the lights went out and my pond stopped working, yes electricity is needed to keep my two cascades working but when the lights returned and the water falls began to pour again I opened my eyes and both my dogs were on the bridge looking at me and more curious even by far most of the fish were all in one little area at the center of the pond I believe all facing were I was, presumably looking at me. I called my dogs and they just stayed for a minute or two before they just came next to me. I wonder what was around me that may have caused the lights to go out and the animals to take note.

I've often wondered if other worlds have people like us so as I've gone on these trips on more than one occasion I've run into souls not of this world so to satisfy my own curiosity I've looked to see what they would look like physically. Remember we can look like anything in this energy based reality so it's hard to see what anyone would really look like. On one occasion I ran into a soul with very broad ideology, what I mean it was open to the concept of this endeavor and was going to sign on for the duration of its lifetime. I asked about its planet; he said that they have been amongst the stars for over a thousand years and have explored many other planets but had never heard of ours. To my surprise they do not share in the same male, family ideology that we do here on earth, for them only specific types would be born to breed and others to explore for example. I wondered about their physical makeup and he explained how they were dwellers of the oceans. Once I showed him about our planet he said we should care for it as it's not the common world to have this type of echo system and many would do much to have such a place. His world was in a distant galaxy from ours so travel to it even at their evolutionary track would not yet be possible. He confirmed how there are many planets inhabited by sentient beings and how the evolution of life was universal. What I mean we are born to learn and evolve as a species and advancement is part of all life. I keep saying he but I'm still not sure the sex thing so I'll continue without diverting from this.

As I continued dialogue with him, it became apparent that ours was one of the lesser evolved fountains of life that were being offered this privilege. Yes, from what I could see what I was being offered was a privilege, so what I still had to be true to me and I'm not sure this is something I'm even capable of fulfilling so why jump into something that might ultimately drag an entire species to extinction. Would I be responsible just by being there to open the eyes of the others out there to our existence. All very scary thoughts and who knows just as I'm having these thoughts what thoughts other beings are having about me. Who knows if others there turn this gift down and decide to come explore us and what if they are not friendly, what if they come to conquer us. Ok, I'm running wild now but I think you get the idea of how stressful this decision is. Curious, one observation, no matter where or what they are another universal truth is we are all spirits of some sort after our physical existence ends.

The biggest eye opener here for me is how time does not work the same, I'm not sure if this is some other dimension or a kind of in between time type of issue. I'm not sure but I've stayed days over there and when I return its but minutes here on earth. Wow, mind blowing stuff and I'm in the middle of all this, what to do with all this information is the reason I'm writing it down. I hope it helps me make sense of all of it. Another thing, I don't seem to get hungry and when I return I'm not agitated or hungry either so this reality does not seem to affect my body but yet they said if I die or something happens to me while there my body on earth will die. Now that I finally got my life to a manageable state I could lose it, but I know from what I do that this or any of a number of lives I have had or will have are nothing in the eternal life of my soul.

One thing is for sure my talents would grow exponentially; I would learn other sorts of magic or how to use it better so this would help my job here immensely. Finally some good news, can you imagine the things I would learn and since they said it would not bother my life here I would or could learn a lifetime in minutes and apply it to my reality later. Communication there is mental and we can all understand each other, the way we all think might be different but mentally we are compatible in the sense that we can understand what we are stating and even our thoughts were open so I've had to hold back our typically ramped thoughts. Can you imagine if here on earth all could hear our thoughts, no we are not ready for such advanced methods of communications yet.

Ok, it's 3 am and I could not go to sleep, I've decided not to do this thing. Maybe a mistake but I have enough with the life that I have now and living this dual life would take its toll. I'm in my fifties and I should if anything do better about taking care of my own health and growth as a family man and leave these other things to younger men. Right now the world and all the stuff going on seem smaller after this experience. I look at what we have and see wonder in all creation, we are not alone but we are unique in the cosmos of this universe and maybe others as well. I've been up for several hours and realize that I have a busy day tomorrow so I should get some sleep. I'm calmer now and I feel rested just from making this decision.

It's been a month or so since the last time I sat down to write, many things have happened in my life, we took our youngest to a family trip in N.Y. City. She wanted this for her 15s birthday so we all did it. She wanted snow and this January was the coldest in over 20 years, even snowed as it dipped to 15 below zero. Well it seems like they are done with me since no more visits and to tell you the truth I'm glad I wrote this stuff down as time passes it becomes more and more difficult to remember the details. That was one of the deals I made with my spirits, as I did this work and dealt with many people I wanted to forget it and not keep any of it. So true to their word I have that capability to let it go so if I do not write it down slowly it just disappears from my mind.

It's a new month and all is well, no more messages or communications from that group of spirits; true to their word as they told me it's a choice and if I decide not to do it then they would just leave me to my life here on this our planet earth. I have many new projects for this year and I feel rejuvenated as those experiences have definitely broadened my view of life in general. I want to have some goals this year like all of us I'm not getting any younger so one of my goals is to get fit again. I've always worked out and I want to recapture those days; I'm a goal person so I have to find a purpose in order to achieve the desire level of fitness. Remember is it impossible or untried, we explore and discover, stretch the boundaries of your limits and realize limitless is more likely your boundaries!

I want to include a few words for my wife in this upcoming Valentine's Day. Nothing is immortalized like writing so I feel to include them would in yet another way show my resolve to our life together, happy valentine's day!

In this fast paced world, we should always beware of the barrenness of a busy life; fulfillment is a broad stroke in any canvas, its color is love, so as you paint your masterpiece never forget the magical colors of Love!

Sharing is caring, so I would share in every instant the passion you light in my soul, though my thirst is quenched by your lips, the instant I look upon your beauty my heart wants to drink that Kool-Aid called your soul again and again my eternal fire burns for you!

The greatest stimulant is the passion you bear, irresistible to me, no mere human can resist standing near the fire and be consumed by the desire I feel for you my wife!

If by falling in love I'll be showing my naked passion, so be it, care not what others think, for I would rather be thought a fool, I would become unbreakable to others and weather any storm, just to be close to you; so in this 2014 valentine's day may your right hand always be stretch out with love, never with need or want for it!

A story written in the heavens that rocked my world to the core, you and I were the characters, we were surrounded by soft mist, raindrops like morning dew on your hair, under the pale moonlight and the fire sun sky, your breath like the wind caught my interest, our language was love, your lips drew me like the moth to the flame, until the roaring inferno that is my passion for you like a volcano erupted shaking the heavens and the earth, such is the story of our love!

To God, love is all about the possible, Impossible only in another's mind, you said I would love you until the end of our time, never grieve for the end, although one has departed we would rejoice in the day we'd meet again; only then would we be at peace, for in the world of the living we had everything and the brief moment in wait where life had no meaning I knew would be quenched as we reunite at heaven's gate!

If time with you would be but a brief instant, I would ride your tears, they are after all conceived in your heart, born of your eyes, live on your cheeks and die on your loving lips, ah to savor the tears of love!